Say Again, Please

Guide to Radio Communications

by **Bob Gardner**

Aviation Supplies & Academics, Inc.
Newcastle, Washington

a Focus Series Book

Say Again, Please – Guide to Radio Communications
Bob Gardner

ASA-SAP
ISBN 1-56027-224-4

Aviation Supplies & Academics, Inc.
Newcastle, Washington

Printed in the United States of America

99 98 97   9 8 7 6 5 4 3

Photo and Illustration Credits: Aerial views of Washington State airports, courtesy Washington State Department of Transportation, Aviation Division; cover photos, ASA, Inc.; p.2-2, p.2-3, Bendix/King; p.2-5 through 2-11, Telex Communications, Inc.; p.2-10 (left), ASA, Inc.; 2-11 (top), Sigtronics; p.2-13 (top) King Silver Crown; p.2-13 (bottom), Terra; p.2-15, Narco Avionics; p.3-2, 3-4, 3-6, 6-1, 10-3, Bob Gardner; p.3-11, Henry Geijsbeek; p.6-7 Olympia airport guide, courtesy Airguide Publications, Inc.

Library of Congress Cataloging-in-Publication Data:

Gardner, Bob, 1928-
    Say again, please : guide to radio communications / by Bob Gardner.
        p.   cm.
    "A Focus series book."
    Includes index.
    ISBN 1-56027-224-4
    1. Radio in aeronautics. I. Title.
  TL693.G34 1995
  629.132'51—dc20
                                                 95-22588
                                                 CIP

Contents

About the Author

Bob Gardner has long been an admired member of the aviation community. He began his flying career as a hobby in Alaska in 1960 while in the U.S. Coast Guard.

Bob's shore-duty assignments in the USCG were all electronic/ communications based. He served in the Communications Division at Coast Guard Headquarters and was Chief of Communications for the Thirteenth Coast Guard District. He holds a Commercial Radiotelephone Operator's license and an Advanced Class Amateur Radio Operator's License.

By 1966, Bob accomplished his Private land and sea, Commercial, instrument, Instructor, CFII and MEL. Over the next 16 years he was an instructor, charter pilot, designated examiner, freight dog and Director of ASA Ground Schools.

Currently, Bob holds an Airline Transport Pilot Certificate with single- and multi-engine land ratings; a CFI certificate with instrument and multi-engine ratings; and a Ground Instructor's Certificate with advanced and instrument ratings. In addition, Bob is a Gold Seal Flight Instructor and has been instructing since 1968. He was recently awarded Flight Instructor of the Year in Washington State. To top off this impressive list of accomplishments, Bob is also a well-known author, journalist and airshow lecturer.

He can be contacted on the Internet at 72247.2617@compuserve.com.

Books by Bob Gardner:
The Complete Private Pilot, Seventh Edition
The Complete Private Pilot syllabus
The Complete Private Pilot Workbook
The Complete Multi-Engine Pilot
The Complete Advanced Pilot

Introduction

We live in a technological age. It is possible to fly without radios or electronic aids to navigation and rely solely on the Mark I eyeball, but there is no question that safety is enhanced when pilots can locate one another beyond visual range. The avionics industry continues to provide pilots with improved products which make communication easier and more reliable, but technology alone is not enough — the user must feel comfortable with the equipment and the system.

We all feel comfortable with the telephone, and an increasing number of pilots feel comfortable with radios that operate in the citizen's or amateur radio bands. However, if there is a controller on the other end of the conversation many pilots freeze up. The goal of this book is to increase your comfort level when using an aircraft radio by explaining how the system works and giving examples of typical transmissions.

A brief word of explanation. I am a flight instructor, and flight instructors talk, and talk, and talk. It is impossible for me to shut off my flight instructor instincts and convert myself totally into a writer. You will pick up on this right away because I repeat myself. Over 30 years of instructing I have learned that if something is repeated in different contexts it will be remembered, so you can count on the same information showing up in more than one chapter. That is not sloppy editing or carelessness, it is good instructional technique. Also, some types of airspace change classification when the tower closes down or the weather observer goes home — there will be some overlap as I discuss each situation in the chapter on each type of airspace.

Conventions

I will not spell out numbers in this text; the AIM says that numerals are to be pronounced individually: 300 is spoken as "three zero zero," runway 13 as "runway one three," etc. I know that I can count on you to make the mental conversion. Altitudes are handled differently, as you will learn in Chapter 3. Also, controllers do not say "degrees" when assigning courses and headings, so neither will I.

In radio communication, the different classes of airspace are spoken as their phonetic equivalents (again, see Chapter 3), without the word "class":

"Cessna 1357X is cleared to enter the Delta surface area..."

In the text, however, they will be referred to as Class B, Class G, etc.

Editor's Note

The examples of radio talk between pilots, controllers and other communications facilities in this text are printed in a bold, non-serif typeface. These are also identified by small labels, which are sometimes abbreviated, as visual aids to the reader to show who is talking. Definitions for these labels can be found in Appendix A, "Communications Facilities."

Example:

PILOT **"Cessna 1357X requests runway 23."**

Acknowledgements

The author wishes to acknowledge the assistance of the following experts in reviewing the text for accuracy and completeness:

Suzanne Alexander, Manager, Boeing Field Tower
Jim Davis, Plans and Procedures, Seattle-Tacoma TRACON
Terry Hall, American Avionics, Seattle
Mike Ogami, Seattle Automated Flight Service Station

Note about the examples used in this book:
The National Aeronautics and Space Administration (NASA) commissions contractors to search the NASA database for lessons to be learned from accidents and pilot reports. Also, NASA publishes *Callback*, a free monthly newsletter that provides its subscribers with selected incidents from the Aviation Safety Reporting System (ASRS). Except for those few cases where I received an anecdote directly from an ATC controller, the examples in this book come from NASA sources.

If you want to receive *Callback*, simply send your address to ASRS, Box 189, Moffett Field, California, 94035.

Note about the airplanes used in this book:
Baron 1014W and Piper 70497 are owned by Dave Sclair, publisher of *General Aviation News and Flyer*. I appreciate his letting me fly his airplanes around the country vicariously in this book. Piper 497 is a J-3 Cub with no electrical system, so I have attempted to ascribe all of the really bonehead errors to it. Cessna 1357X does not exist.

1 The ABCs of Communicating

The Pilot-Controller Partnership For Safety

Aviation communication is a team effort, not a competition between pilots and controllers. Air traffic controllers are just as anxious as you are for your flight to be completed safely. They will cooperate with you whenever they can do so and still remain *consistent with safety*. They are not the equivalent of the stereotypical law enforcement officer just waiting for you to do something wrong. They hate paperwork as much as anyone, and filing a violation against a pilot starts an avalanche of forms and reports. On the other hand, they have a tremendous amount of responsibility and can be severely overloaded with traffic; that means that you can't expect a controller to ignore everyone else in order to give you special treatment.

Doing Things by the Book

The controller's actions are bound by FAA Handbook 7110.65, the *Air Traffic Control Manual*. That publication tells controllers exactly what phraseology to use in virtually every situation, and woe to the controller who has had a slip of the tongue when he or she sits down with a supervisor to jointly monitor tapes during a quarterly evaluation. That is not to say that the controller operates in a procedural straitjacket. If you don't understand what a controller has said, or do understand but don't know what you are being told to do, just say "I don't understand," or words to that effect. The controller won't be out pounding the pavement, since the intent of the communication was to extend a helping hand and make your life a little easier.

As a pilot, you do not have a manual of canned phrases that are expected to meet every situation. The *Aeronautical Information Manual* contains a section on communication procedure, and if you read it (and you should) you will receive guidance on the best way to get your message across to the controller.

Both the *Aeronautical Information Manual* (AIM) and the *Air Traffic Control Manual* contain the Pilot/Controller Glossary. The intent of the Glossary is to ensure that certain words have the same meaning to both the pilot and the controller. Before you ask your instructor a question like "What does 'resume own navigation' mean?" look it up in the Pilot/Controller Glossary. There are very few terms used in normal aviation communication that do not appear in the Glossary.

Figure 1-1. AIM and ATC Handbook

A historical sidelight: The Pilot/Controller Glossary didn't exist before 1974. It became apparent only after a major airline accident that some phrases meant one thing to controllers and something entirely different to pilots, and the glossary was born. A very good reason for you to familiarize yourself with the P/C Glossary in the AIM.

Can't We All Just Get Along?

An important part of the teamwork concept is negotiation. Many pilots, both novices and old hands, think that a directive from an air traffic controller must be obeyed without question. Those pilots have forgotten that the Federal Aviation Regulations (FARs) make the pilot-in-command of the airplane solely responsible for the safety of the flight. A controller cannot direct you to do something that is unsafe or illegal. You must remember that you are almost always in a better position to determine the safety of a given action than the controller is.

For example, let's assume that you are flying in Class B airspace (to be defined later). In that type of airspace the controller can give you specific altitudes and/or headings to fly; you are required by FAR §91.123 to comply with those clearances. When the controller says "Turn right to 330" and you can see that to do so would take you too close to a cloud, it becomes your responsibility to say "Unable due to weather." After all, the controller can't see clouds on the radar screen and has no way of knowing that you would be turning toward a cloud. FAR §91.3 says that you are the final authority as to operation of your aircraft and that supersedes all other regulations.

Another example: You have just touched down on the runway and the controller says "Turn right at the next taxiway." If you are rolling too fast to make the turn without wearing a big flat spot on your main landing gear and overheating the brakes, it is your responsibility to say "Unable." If you are really busy with the airplane, don't say anything until you can reach for the microphone without losing directional control.

Other situations where negotiation might be used include being assigned a landing runway that requires a lot of taxiing to get to your destination or, in light winds, a departure runway that takes you in a direction that you don't want to go. Simply say,

PILOT **"Cessna 1357X requests runway 23"**

(instead of runway 14, for example). If the change can be accomplished without affecting either your safety or that of other flights, your request will be granted. There are almost as many exceptions to the rules as there are rules, but too many pilots simply go by the rules without attempting negotiation.

Mike Fright

We are all afraid of saying the wrong thing, especially when dozens of other people are listening. Aviation magazines frequently print stories of humorous communication mistakes or misunderstandings. In aviation, it is far more important to say something than to keep quiet and proceed into a potentially tight situation — especially when traveling at two miles a minute.

Call-in talk shows are quite common on both radio and television, and the callers are in the same situation as you are when you pick up the microphone in your airplane as a "first-time caller" — thousands of people will be able to hear their "er's" and "uh's." The difference is that their safety and that of others does not depend on their making that call — yours does.

Technobabble Not Spoken Here

Use plain English. "Tell me what you want me to do" might not appear in the AIM, but if it is necessary to use that phrase, it gets the job done. The following suggestion will be repeated later more than once, because it is important: Listen to your radio. Other airplanes will be talking to ATC, getting weather reports, or communicating with advisory services. The information they are receiving might be useful to you and make it unnecessary for you to make a transmission (or allow you to drastically shorten your transmission). Go to any small airport (one without a control tower) with a VHF receiver that covers the aviation frequencies and just monitor the airport's Common

Traffic Advisory Frequency (CTAF) — ask one of the local pilots if you aren't sure what the CTAF for that airport is. You will hear a dozen airplanes reporting that

C they are landing or taking off on runway 14 (for example), and then a strange voice will come on the frequency and ask "What runway is in use?" That pilot hasn't learned to listen.

That VHF receiver is your best source of information on how to communicate as a pilot. Get a copy of the Airport/Facility Directory (A/FD) for your area and look up the frequencies that are used by the local airports and air traffic control facilities. Look in the back of the directory for Air Route Traffic Control Center (ARTCC) frequencies, then tune in and listen to how the airliners communicate when en route. You will hear lots of good examples and a few alarmingly bad examples. You may not be able to hear both ends of the communication unless you live within line-of-sight distance of the ground station's antenna, but a visit to a local tower-controlled airport will eliminate that problem.

Licensing

Any U.S.-registered airplane you fly must have an FCC radio station license if it has a transmitting device installed. You can have all the receivers you want, but to transmit, a station license is required. It should be in a little side pocket in the cockpit, together with the registration and airworthiness certificates, and should show the name and address of the airplane's registered owner.

To use an installed aircraft radio in the United States, you don't have to have any kind of operator's license. Travel to Canada or Mexico, however, and you will be expected to carry a Third Class Restricted Radiotelephone operator's license. Any Federal Communications Commission office can issue one if you promise to avoid saying bad words on the air. An FCC commercial license is even better than a Third Class Restricted license, but an amateur radio license is no good on aircraft frequencies. Keep in mind that you won't even get into a hassle about an operator's license unless you are outside of the good old U.S.A. and subject to another country's laws.

Handheld transmitter-receivers (to be called transceivers from here on) are very popular for emergency use. If you are flying an airplane with its own station license, that license covers the handheld. You will use the airplane registration number as an identifier. If you want to use a handheld in an airplane without a station license, however, you will have to apply to the FCC for a "mobile" license, which will assign an identifier to the handheld — something like "N12345MOB."

Don't look to the Federal Aviation Regulations for anything about how radios are to be used — that is the sole province of the FCC.

Figure 1-2. FCC license application

Hello, Operator?

Cellular phones are becoming more and more popular, and many pilots use their cellular phones in business. What could be better than calling that hot prospect from 12,500 feet and setting up a lunch date? The hard fact is that doing so would violate FCC (not FAA) regulations. The cellular phone system is designed to be used on the surface, where callers are automatically switched from one small cell to another as they travel. From 12,500 feet or any other altitude, the signal from your phone might activate a dozen cells at once, and that is frowned upon by the FCC. To make matters worse, when you use your cell phone it transmits enough identifying information (for billing purposes) for the FCC enforcement officers to easily prove a violation.

There are approved airborne telephones — ask at your local avionics shop. And there are entrepreneurs who are working with the FCC on approval of a cellular network specifically for airborne cell phones. The network will probably use different frequencies than you use with your cell phone today, so watch and wait.

Can you use your cell phone on the ground to call for gas or file a flight plan? Absolutely.

By the way, leave your cell phone in your luggage while on an air carrier. Even if you want to use it on the ground, you may find that the flight attendants will not permit you to do so. The FARs make the captain the final authority on the use of portable electronic equipment, and there are documented instances of cell phones interfering with air carrier avionics while in the receive mode.

2 Understanding Your Equipment

Look At All Those Knobs and Buttons!

When you had your first flight lesson, your instructor probably went to great lengths to tell you how to read the instruments and how to use the controls. During that and subsequent lessons the proper use of the radios and their controls were most likely glossed over. After all, what can be difficult about selecting a frequency and picking up a microphone? If the airplane had an audio control panel or an intercommunication system, it is possible that the instructor set them up and their use was taken for granted (my apologies to all instructors to whom these generalities do not apply).

If you did all of your training in one airplane, let's say a Cessna 152, the first time you got into a different 152 the odds are that the radio setup was different. Or when you got your license and checked out in a larger airplane, its radio installation was different than the one in the 152. At a fixed-base operation that uses airplanes leased back from individual owners, the radio installation in each airplane will be tailored to meet the requirements of the owner, not the FBO.

Communications hardware can be confusing. It would be impossible to describe all of the possible combinations you might encounter, and if I attempted to do so my discussion would be out of date in six months. Another complicating factor is conversion of old, mechanically tuned radios to the new digital displays. It's hard to stay ahead of avionics technology. I can, however, give you a general overview of communications hardware.

Transceivers

A typical aircraft nav-comm is shown in Figure 2-1; the navigation function will be ignored in this text. Your aircraft radio transmits and receives on frequencies between 118.000-136.975 MHz (the display of 136.97 in Figure 2-1 is 136.970; you get 136.975 by pulling the knob marked "PULL 25K). There is no .005 display until you get into really sophisticated airplanes with cathode-ray tube displays. Whether or not it has .25 MHz spacing will depend on its age.

Many older radios were designed for .50 MHz spacing (118.000, 118.500, etc.) but the need for new frequencies has forced many ATC facilities to use frequencies with .25 MHz spacing with no alternatives. If you are told to switch to 135.525 and your radio can select only 135.500 and 135.550, you are going to have to say "Unable" to the controller. The requirement for 760 channels (.25 MHz spacing) is largely limited to Air Route Traffic Control Centers (ARTCC) as of mid-1995, but you can expect it to filter down to towers and terminal radar facilities.

Other than selecting the correct frequency, there is little you can do to a transmitter. Radio manufacturers have made great technological advances since microprocessors became available, and one improvement with a large impact in this discussion is frequency storage. Note that two frequencies are displayed on the comm side of Figure 2-1: the top one is the active frequency, and the bottom one is the stand-by frequency, and if you push the button on the left, 136.97 would jump up to the top and become the active frequency.

If the radio in the airplane you are flying has mechanical frequency display — white numbers on a black background that flip over like a speedometer as you turn the frequency selection control — you don't have storage capability. With this mechanical type of frequency selection you can turn the frequency selector clockwise from

Figure 2-1. Nav-comm transceiver

118.000 to 136.900, but a mechanical stop prevents you from going any further. With digital tuners you can go right through 136.900, and the display starts over again at 118.000. This is not only a timesaver but saves wear and tear on the mechanical linkages as well.

Digital displays, those orange-on-black, green-on-black, or black-on-white segmented numerals that have become so common in everyday life, tell you that your transmitter/receiver probably has frequency storage and flip-flop capability. The simplest arrangement is typified by the KY-96A, which has no navigation receiver to confuse the issue (Figure 2-2).

A transceiver with flip-flop capabilities such as the KY-96A allows you to select a new frequency on the standby side while transmitting and receiving on the frequency shown on the active side. You might have the tower frequency selected (or stored) on the standby side while using the ground control frequency on the active side. Radios similar to the KY-96A can store many frequencies (nine, in the case of the KY-96A) to be called up at the push of the CHAN button. You can always stay one step ahead if you have some idea of what the next frequency to be selected will be, and you can cycle through the stored frequencies with that button.

Another variation on frequency storage doesn't use a flip-flop but lets you choose three or four frequencies that are selectable by a switch; at an airport in Class D airspace, you might have the ATIS (Automated Terminal Information Service — to be defined later) in position 1, ground control in position 2, and the tower frequency in position 3. As soon as you have received the ATIS information on position 1 and have switched to position 2 for taxi instructions, you can retune position 1 to departure control, UNICOM, or whatever frequency you plan to use after leaving the Class airspace.

Figure 2-2. KY-96A transceiver

Squelch

The squelch control permits you to fly along in blessed silence without having the continuous roar of static in your ears. The only time any sound will reach your ears is when a receiver signal is strong enough to overcome the squelch setting or "break squelch."

Many newer radios have an automatic squelch which is set by your radio shop. Older radios will have a squelch knob, and this is how you use it: Turn the squelch knob until static assaults your eardrums, set the volume to a comfortable level, then turn the squelch knob until the static is silenced — the correct setting is right on the edge of squelch break. If you turn the squelch knob beyond that point, you establish a squelch level that is too high for incoming signals to exceed before you can hear them.

Radios with automatic squelch will have a selector switch with a "pull-to-test" position that bypasses the squelch control (Figures 2-1 and 2-2). This is valuable for setting a comfortable audio level, but it also has a more practical use. What if you are 75 miles away from your destination airport and want to check on the weather and the runway in use? Chances are that the ATIS signal will be too weak to break squelch at that distance. However, if you select the "test" position you may be able to decipher the ATIS through the background of static.

Many newer radios have an illuminated "T" next to the transmitter frequency when you are talking on that radio. It tells you that your transmitter is working, of course, but it is also a warning that your transmitter may have been keyed accidentally.

The microprocessor brought with it miniaturization, and miniaturization means that it is possible to put more avionics goodies in a panel than were possible in the past. This is good. Solid-state devices don't put out as much heat as vacuum tubes did, and that is also good. However, solid-state devices such as transistors and micro-processors are very temperature-sensitive, and that is bad. It means that your radio stack will probably require one or more cooling fans or ram air from outside. There is also the possibility that your solid-state equipment contains a thermal shutoff device that will remove the power from some of your avionics if the temperature gets too high. Talk this over with someone from the avionics shop that services the airplane so that you know which pieces of equipment might be affected. It's much less expensive to install a cooling fan than it is to have your radios in the shop constantly.

Mikes

Unless you are an amateur radio operator, a user of the Citizen's Band, or a radio announcer, it is likely that the microphone in your trainer airplane will be the first mike you have used. All microphones perform the same function — turning your voice into electrical waves — but they differ in how they accomplish this task.

The microphone found in most trainers is a carbon mike (Figure 2-3). It works exactly like a telephone handset in that it contains a little canister of carbon granules. One side of the canister is a thin diaphragm that vibrates as the sound waves from your mouth hit it. This vibration changes the electrical resistance of the granules and thereby varies the current flowing through it. That's as technical as we need to get. That semi-technical explanation gives you some insight into how you can get the most out of your relatively inexpensive carbon mike.

First, you have to be sure that you hold the mike directly in front of your mouth so that the amplitude of your voice's sound waves is fully utilized — you can't talk across a carbon mike or speak into one from several inches away and expect great results. Most carbon mikes have a little protrusion that you should press against your lip to make sure that the granules get all shook up as you speak. Talking into the back of the microphone accomplishes absolutely nothing, yet every year, lots of pilots try it.

Second, it is possible for the granules to stick together (humidity? cigarette smoke?) and not vibrate as much as they should. This is not a common problem, but if you are holding the mike properly and speaking into it distinctly and still get reports that your voice is weak, gently rapping the mike on a hard surface might help. Please don't do this while keying the microphone — you don't want to damage other pilots' eardrums. Carbon mikes can withstand a certain amount of physical abuse; that explains why they are so often found in trainers. The other side of the coin is that the granules can vibrate only so much. When you yell into the microphone your voice doesn't get louder at the receiver end, it just gets distorted. If you live in New York and call California on the telephone, do you yell because your voice has to travel so far? Yelling into any kind of microphone is counterproductive.

Figure 2-3. Carbon microphone

Stepping up in class, there are dynamic mikes (Figure 2-4), crystal mikes, electret mikes, and condenser mikes. There may be a few more by the time you read this book. These share a common characteristic: they don't react well to physical abuse. It is that same sensitivity that makes them valuable in a noisy cockpit. It is not important for you to know how these mikes work. Suffice it to say that speaking into one in a conversational tone will produce a readable signal at the receiver.

All handheld microphones have a push-to-talk (PTT) switch (in Figure 2-4, the PTT is on the front and you talk into the top). True to its name, you have to push the switch ("key the mike") to transmit, and release it to receive. A common error among neophytes who expect a radio to act like a telephone is to push the button and then hold it down after completing their transmission. You can't hear while you are transmitting because the receiver is blocked, so maybe they should be renamed PTTRTR switches: Push to talk, release to receive.

As you sit in the cockpit of the typical single-engine airplane you are surrounded by noise. The engine does its noisy thing, the propeller sends waves of air back to vibrate the windshield, and if there are any airleaks around the doors or windows they will add a noise like a banshee's wail. On the receiver end, the controller or pilot must somehow distinguish your voice from the background noise. Fortunately, almost all microphones are designed to be noise-canceling. That is, they are extremely sensitive in the direction of your mouth and they are designed to internally cancel noise coming from anywhere else. That's another reason for you to be sure that the business end of the microphone is very close to your lips.

Figure 2-4. Dynamic microphone

Speakers

Almost every airplane has a speaker installed in the headliner so that people in the front seats can hear. More often than not, it is a very small speaker and not of the highest quality. If that speaker fails you will have a very real loss of two-way communication capability. One of the things you should check before takeoff is the presence of headphones that you can use in case the speaker dies. They don't have to be the most expensive headphones on the market, just something to get you back on the ground safely. Don't bring your stereo headphones from home — they won't work.

Silence from the speaker could be caused by failure of the audio amplifier required to drive it. This amp could be a separate unit, included with the audio switch panel, it could be part of your nav-comm receiver, or it could be a stand-alone unit. The important thing to remember is that the speaker can suddenly fall silent, and you should have a backup method of listening to your communications radios. When you use the headphone jack and/or throw the switches on the audio panel from SPKR to PHONE, you bypass the audio amplifier, thus the need for headphones to back up the speaker.

Headphones

Figures 2-5 and 2-6 show two types of headphones, and you should know that there are several other types not illustrated. Do you like to hear slightly muffled engine noise or do you want blessed silence? The difference might be several hundred dollars. Do you want to hear ATC with one ear while monitoring the passengers, and the cabin speaker with the other? The EarSet® (Figure 2-5) is one solution; you can get a separate boom mike that hooks onto your sunglasses. Passengers may be concerned when the pilot puts on a big headset (Figure 2-7) and effectively goes into seclusion during the flight: "Did you hear that noise, Mabel? The pilot couldn't have heard it and I think the wing is

Figure 2-5. Earset® receiver with earloop

Figure 2-6. Lightweight headphones

falling off!" It's also a major drag for the instructor when the student is using muff-type headphones and there is no mike or phone connection on the right side of the cockpit. They will be able to communicate through gestures and shouting, but it won't be easy.

The amount of cushioning around the earpiece, and therefore the amount of cabin noise/conversation you can monitor, varies quite a bit. Try several types, but be warned — over a flying career you will probably buy two or three headsets of different types. Most headsets have their own volume controls, so if each occupant of a pilot seat is wearing a headset the volumes can be controlled individually. With a volume control on the receiver, one on the intercom, and another on the headset, there should be sufficient control to satisfy everyone.

Boom Microphones

You won't be flying very long before you decide that reaching for a handheld micro-phone and returning it to its holder is a lot of trouble and distraction. You don't solve this problem by sticking the mike under your thigh where you can get at it easily. More often than not, pilots who do that key the mike by shifting around in their seat, and for the next several minutes every word said in the cockpit is transmitted to hundreds of ears. While they are sitting on the mike and blithely transmitting their life story to the world at large, other pilots are unable to contact controllers, controllers are unable to contact other pilots, and a large number of people are getting very angry at the thoughtless pilot. Sometime during the conversation someone is bound to say the aircraft's N-number, making it all too easy for the FAA, the FCC, and an army of angry pilots to identify the miscreant.

The best way to solve the distraction problem is with a boom mike (Figures 2-7 through 2-10). If you are just beginning your flight training and your instructor insists that you use a boom mike, you have a very smart instructor. Garth Brooks uses a boom mike. Madonna uses a boom mike. Michael Jackson uses a boom mike. Telephone operators in TV commercials use boom mikes. I'm sure that you have noticed that in every case mentioned above, the business end of the mike is positioned either directly

Figure 2-8

Figure 2-7. Headset with volume control
and boom mike

in front of the performer's mouth or very close to that centered position. You've probably also noticed that Garth's, Madonna's, and Jackson's mikes are surrounded by foam plastic windsleeves to keep extraneous noises from being picked up. It is possible but not probable that your airplane's boom mike will have a similar sleeve — almost all aviation boom mikes are extremely directional.

The boom portion of a boom mike can be swiveled and adjusted to put the mike right where you want it. One word of caution: Before you bite into an apple or a sandwich, swing the mike out of the way or that first bite will be mostly plastic. Another word of caution: If someone calls you while you are eating lunch and the boom mike is somewhere up near your forehead, swing it back into position before you key the mike and reply. I speak from experience.

Earphones with foam covers that fit over the ear but do not enclose it (Figure 2-8), and earpieces that actually fit into the ear canal (Figure 2-10) should be considered. Some pilots like to have one ear covered while they listen to ATC, while monitoring the cabin speaker, the passengers, and engine sounds with the other ear (just about any kind of earplug will protect your hearing while you do this). Your best bet is a visit to the local avionics shop where you can try all kinds of headsets to determine which suits you best.

Figure 2-9

Figure 2-10

You will be able to hear your own voice very faintly when transmitting while using a headset. This is called "sidetone," and if you don't hear it you may not be transmitting.

If the boom mike is continually in front of your mouth, where is the PTT switch? One of two places. If the owner of the airplane has had one installed, the PTT switch will be on the horn of the yoke, either directly under your thumb or on the front side under your index finger. Very

Figure 2-11. PTT switch

convenient. But what if you are a renter who shows up at the airplane with a headset in a bag only to learn that the airplane does not have an installed PTT switch? Back to the avionics shop. PTT switches that can be temporarily attached to the yoke with hook-and-loop tape (Figure 2-11) are not too expensive and it doesn't make sense to buy a headset and not pop for a PTT switch, just in case. The headphone plug from your headset goes into the airplane's headset jack, the mike plug from your headset goes into the PTT adapter, and the mike plug from the PTT switch goes to the airplane's mike jack. Attach the PTT to the yoke where it is convenient to a finger with your hand in its normal flying position, and you are in business.

Intercoms

Intercommunication systems are becoming common in the general aviation fleet — the days of students and instructors trying to yell over the noise of a piston engine will soon be behind us. The ideal situation is an intercom that is permanently installed in the panel, but portable intercoms best fit the needs of renters. Once again, the intercoms in Figures 2-12 and 2-13 represent only a sampling of what is available.

In addition to the standard function of allowing both front seat occupants to either key the transmitter or converse with one another in normal tones, intercoms can bring the back seat passengers into the loop or provide them with musical entertainment. Another useful feature is a tape recorder output that allows you to tape your lessons and review them at your leisure. Some upscale intercom systems allow either the passengers or everyone on board to listen to music, automatically muting the music when a transmission is received.

When you plug the mike and headphone connectors from your headset to the intercom's input jacks and then plug the intercom's connectors to the airplane jacks, the possibility increases that a loose connection might cause problems. If the receivers seem unusually quiet, or if you transmit and no one answers, check the connections first.

Figures 2-12 and 2-13. Portable intercoms

Some intercoms have a VOX (voice-operated) control, while with other systems it is automatic. VOX allows you to set a voltage level that permits your voice to be heard on the system but does not allow the system to be triggered by engine noise; it is used when the pilots want to talk to one another or to the passengers. It is adjusted by talking into the boom mike while adjusting the VOX until you can hear your own sidetone voice in your headset. Everyone plugged into the intercom system should be able to converse with this setting. With most systems, when either front seat occupant pushes the PTT switch, all of the mikes are live and a rear seat passenger might inadvertently ask ATC to pass the mustard. This possibility is eliminated when a "crew/passenger" switch is present and in the "crew" position. Your avionics shop will have a demonstration panel to show you how to use all of the unit's functions.

Audio Panels

Virtually every modern airplane has some form of audio switch panel (Figures 2-14 and 2-15) that allows you to switch between the cabin speaker and the headphones, or listen to two frequencies at once. (American Avionics will not install two radios unless an audio switch panel is included in the installation.) The switch panel will include a microphone selector switch for you to use when you have been talking on your #1 radio and want to talk on #2. If you fail to switch transmitters you will, of course, transmit on the wrong frequency:

PILOT "Dallas Tower, Baron 1014W ready for takeoff."

GROUND "14W, you're still on ground control."

PILOT "Sorry about that!"

This is a mistake that even the most experienced pilots make, so don't feel bad if you do. But be more careful next time. Figure 2-14 provides for two transmitters, and when you select a transmitter its receiver is automatically selected. The SPKR push button is a toggle — it switches from speaker to headphone and back again. The BOTH position allows you to monitor the receiver of Comm 2 when you have the MIC 1 button pushed and are capable of talking and receiving on Comm 1.

The switches on panels like Figure 2-15 have a center "off" position, and if you are not careful to select either "speaker" or "phone," and leave the switch centered, you will not hear anything at all.

The panel in Figure 2-15 has an "auto" position. When the switches for both Comm 1 and Comm 2 are in the "off" position and the "auto" switch is in the speaker position, the output to the speaker is automatically switched from receiver 1 to receiver 2 when

Figure 2-14 and 2-15. Audio panels

you change the transmitter switch from C1 to C2. If the "auto" switch is in the phone position, of course, the receiver output will go to the headphones. This makes it unnecessary for you to continually fiddle with the Comm 1 and Comm 2 switches.

There will be times when you will want to have (for example) Comm 1 set to the tower frequency while simultaneously listening to the ATIS on Comm 2. That can mean two signals coming into your ears at one time, but just keep your finger on the Comm 2 switch and you can turn it off when you are called by the tower.

The major advantage of audio switch panels is the ability to switch between navigation and communication radios without constantly fiddling with the volume and squelch controls. Once you have set the volume and squelch to a comfortable level you can leave those knobs alone and deal only with the switch panel.

Instructors differ on how to use the audio switch panel with the communications radios. One school of thought advocates using only the #1 radio for communications and using the #2 radio to monitor an ATIS, Flight Watch, 121.5 MHz, or other frequency you choose. This works quite well with radios that have a flip-flop capability because when you switch from one controller to another, the old frequency remains on display so that you can switch back if you are unable to contact the new controller.

The other school of thought advocates switching between the #1 and #2 radios every time you are handed off to another controller. This works well with mechanically-tuned radios that do not have flip-flop capability. When you are handed off from one controller to another and switch radios to accomplish the change, the "old" frequency is still mechanically displayed.

New pilots tend to spend a lot of time looking at the radios while changing frequencies, and this takes their eyes away from the important task of scanning for traffic. You should learn to tune your radios by counting "clicks." Once you have learned how many clicks of rotation it takes to change the frequency one megahertz, turn the frequency selector knob the number of clicks you estimate will get you to the one you want, while keeping your eyes outside of the cockpit. Then, take a quick glance at the radio panel to see how close you have come to the desired frequency. With practice, you will be able to change frequencies with hardly any need to look at the panel. Don't transmit until you have verified that you have selected the correct frequency.

Digital frequency displays do go blank occasionally, making it impossible for you to know what frequency is set in the window. Some manufacturers have an emergency mode that defaults to, say, 118.000. Then you can count the clicks to get to your desired frequency. If you have a digital display, this is something you want to be clear about before you fly with the equipment.

Transponders

Your airplane's transponder consists of a transmitter and receiver, so I can't ignore it in a book about communications. In normal VFR operations the transponder just sits there doing its job, blinking its little heart out while squawking code 1200. Every time it receives an interrogation from an air traffic control radar on the ground it sends out a coded reply. Its reply light may not blink too often when you are flying out in the boondocks where ATC radars are few and far between, but when you approach a busy terminal area it will blink continually.

At the controller's position your airplane will show up as an anonymous data block showing 1200 and, if you have Mode C, your altitude. When you call the controller for VFR flight following and are asked to push the IDENT button (don't hold it, just push it — it stays on for 20 seconds), your data block will intensify on the controller's scope.

If you are given a discrete transponder code to squawk and the controller has the scope set to display a full data block, your return will expand to include your callsign and groundspeed. Important note: When a controller asks you to squawk a discrete code, do not simply set the new code without a verbal acknowledgment; if you do not repeat the new code the controller might assume that you missed the transmission and be forced to take the time to transmit again. It would be a red-letter day at ATC if yours was the only aircraft the controller was working, and the controller cannot divert attention from other aircraft to see if you have responded correctly to

Figure 2-16. Transponder

the new assignment. Even worse, if the controller assigned code 4625 and you mistakenly set your transponder to 4325, your return would not show up on the scope at all and the controller would have to give you a call to find out what happened.

The Aeronautical Information Manual says that you should not inadvertently squawk 7500, 7600, 7700, or 7777 while switching codes. This should be a fairly easy task; when switching from a 4 to a 1, for example, turn the selector counterclockwise to avoid passing 7 on the way. Do not turn the transponder function switch to STBY while changing codes.

Code 7500 tells authorities that there is a hijacker on board; its intentional use by a VFR pilot on a pleasure flight is unlikely. Code 7600 reports to ATC a loss of two-way communications capability and is of primary interest to pilots on instrument flight plans. However, if you are receiving flight following services from ATC and your transmitter or receiver fails, the controller will worry about your failure to reply to advisories — it would be helpful if you would squawk 7600 until you land and can call a Flight Service Station on the telephone.

Of course, you might want to squawk code 7700 on purpose — it is the emergency code that alerts controllers to the fact that you have a problem of some kind. A few seconds spent in setting 7700 into your transponder (while changing tanks and looking for a flat spot on which to land) might save hours of searching by the authorities.

To conform with the regulations you should have your airplane's transponder ON at all times when you are flying in controlled airspace. This can be a real lifesaver, even if you do not avail yourself of VFR flight following, because ATC radar stores the tracks of all transponder returns. It is possible (not a sure thing, unfortunately) that if you turn up missing they will be able to replay the stored data to see where your 1200 squawk terminated. But if you fly so low that no radar can interrogate your transponder, there will be no display on the controller's scope.

"Mode A" on the transponder function switch provides only a target for the controller; "Mode C," or "ALT," adds your altitude to the data block on the ATC radar scope. Does the airplane you are flying have an altitude encoding altimeter? It should, but put the switch in the ALT position ("squawk" altitude) just in case. Like chicken soup for medicinal purposes, it can't hurt.

Where did this "squawk" stuff come from? During World War II, when the "Identification, Friend or Foe" system first used transponders, controllers and pilots called the system the "parrot" in an attempt to fool the enemy. Whether or not the enemy was fooled is subject to question, but today's request to "squawk standby" used to be "strangle your parrot." Only the squawk terminology has survived.

When you set your transponder to 7700, it tells air traffic controllers that you have an emergency of some kind by enhancing your data block on their scope. The FAA takes a very broad view of just what constitutes an emergency — a much broader view than that of most pilots. Any time you are apprehensive as to your safety you should ask for help. Too many pilots will wait until they are almost out of fuel before letting anyone know about their situation.

The best procedure is to ask for radar flight following. If you are in radio contact with ATC for traffic advisories, a word to the controller is all it takes to get help; your position is known and the controller is in direct contact with rescue agencies. No special communication procedure is required.

If you are not in voice contact with ATC, but are monitoring the Air Route Traffic Control frequency for the area in which you are flying (listed in the Airport/Facility Directory), all you have to do is squawk 7700, pick up the mike, and say:

PILOT **"Center, Baron 1014W, emergency [or MAYDAY]"**

…followed by as much detail as you have time for. Believe me, they will be listening for your call, because of the way the 7700 squawk affects their radar scopes. The controller will then get the details of the situation and provide help as required. I strongly recommend that you either ask for flight following, or monitor a Center frequency whenever you fly cross-country.

③ A Matter of Procedure

Why You Have Two Ears and One Mouth

The most important rule of communication is this: Listen before you talk. Aviation radio is a huge party line, with dozens of people involved at any one time. If you switch frequencies and make an immediate transmission without listening first, your transmission may block communication from another airplane. It's not like a telephone, where both parties can talk at once and still hear one another. Several bad things happen when you fail to listen before transmitting: Your transmission may not be heard, another airplane may miss an important transmission because of your carelessness, or two simultaneous transmissions on the same frequency will cause a loud squeal in the headsets of everyone monitoring the frequency.

In normal, day-to-day conversation, if you heard one person ask another "Where do you work?" you wouldn't even consider interrupting with your own question until the first person's question had been answered. You know from experience that a question will elicit a reply, and that to interfere is bad manners. In the world of aviation communication, a transmission may not sound like a question but you should still wait for a reply.

> PILOT "Bigtown Tower, Piper 70497 six miles south for landing with Echo"

— doesn't sound like a question, but you know that the tower is going to give 497 some form of instruction or clearance and that you should not key your mike until the exchange is complete. Always listen for a few seconds before you transmit.

Is this a mistake you could make inadvertently? Unfortunately, it is — and there is nothing you can do about it. The FAA's communication network includes remote transmitter/receivers, and it is possible for a pilot too far away for you to hear to be calling an FAA facility on a remote frequency that you plan to use. If the controller says,

TOWER **"Piper 70497 stand by, you stepped on another transmission,"**

just keep quiet — if the controller can hear both pilots but you can't hear one another, there's nothing for you to feel bad about.

Similarly, you may listen on a frequency for a few seconds, hear nothing going on, and have your call to an FAA facility answered with,

TOWER **"Piper 70497, stand by, I'm working other traffic."**

In this situation, the controller might be talking to a military flight on an ultra-high aviation frequency (UHF) that your radio cannot receive. Those are the breaks of the game.

Never feel that you are doing an ATC facility a favor by not bothering the controllers with a call. The traffic count (number of communications) can affect staffing levels, pay scales, and even the continued existence of a facility.

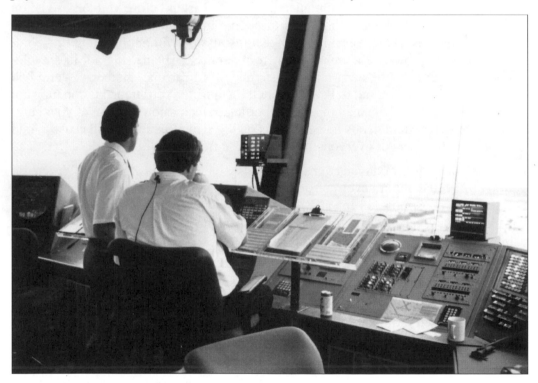

What's In A Name?

Each type of ATC facility is addressed in a specific way. When you call a Flight Service Station, use **Radio**:

> PILOT "**Norfolk Radio, Baron 1014W 15 miles north, request traffic advisory.**"

A call to a control tower uses **Tower**:

> PILOT "**Portland Tower, Baron 1014W ready for takeoff.**"

On the ground at a tower-controlled airport, use **Ground** when calling the ground controller:

> PILOT "**Charlotte Ground, Baron 1014W off runway five, taxi to the ramp.**"

If you are calling a radar controller at an approach/departure facility after being told by a Center or tower controller to contact that facility, just follow instructions:

> CONTROLLER "**Baron 1014W contact Bay Approach 135.4**"

— which should be acknowledged with,

> PILOT "**14W going to approach,**"

and after listening on 135.4 for a few seconds,

> PILOT "**Bay APPROACH, Baron 1014W level at 2,500, VFR.**"

If you are told to call **Departure** Control, of course, that is who you would call. But what if you want to make an initial contact with a radar facility and don't know whether to address it as approach or departure — use either one, or **Radar**:

> PILOT "**Seattle Radar, Piper 70497 over Winslow, 3,500' VFR, request clearance through Class B airspace to Renton,**"

would do the trick. Each one of these facilities will be covered in detail later.

At many airports, airspace sectorization means that when the wind shifts and the active runway changes, a given location might change from approach's airspace to that owned by the departure controller. This kind of thing is just shrugged off by the controller, so don't worry about who to address — they will respond regardless of which name you use.

You will call an Air Traffic Control Center when you want radar flight following on a cross-country trip, and you should address that facility as **Center**:

> PILOT "**Fort Worth Center, Piper 70497 over Blue Ridge VOR, request VFR flight following to Waco.**"

Center frequencies can be found in the Airport/Facility Directory.

A UNICOM station would, of course, be addressed as **UNICOM**.

When you need weather information or want to make a pilot report, use **Flight Watch** on 122.0 MHz (this is only monitored from 0600 until 2200 local time). You will find locations of Flight Watch stations and their remotes on the inside of the back cover of the A/FD.

> PILOT "Houston Flight Watch, Baron 1014W over Lufkin, VFR to Waco, can I have the latest Waco weather?"

Controllers have heard everything, so if you use the wrong name by mistake the controller will usually reply using the proper name without missing a beat.

Say It All in One Breath

When transmitting to ATC, don't add last minute thoughts. For example, if you say:

> PILOT **"Centennial Tower, Baron 1014W ready for takeoff...we're VFR to Grand Junction,"**

there is an excellent chance that the controller will key the mike and begin to reply as soon as you say "takeoff" and pause. The result will be a squeal on the frequency as you and the controller transmit simultaneously, and the controller will miss your comment about your destination.

"Roger, Wilco, Over and Out"

That phrase is often incorrectly used as an example of communication overkill. There is no question that with the sophistication of today's radios, "over" and "out" are pretty much outdated. However, the terms **Roger** and **Wilco** still play an important part in communications with ATC.

You would never know it from listening to your VHF radio, but Roger is a term that should be used very infrequently. It simply means "I have received your transmission," and nothing more. It does not mean "yes" or "I will comply." For example, if the tower controller says,

> TOWER **"Piper 70497, you are number two for takeoff,"**

you can reasonably reply "Roger," because it would be foolish to say "yes" or "I will comply." If a controller asks if you are over the blue water tower, however, your answer should be "affirmative," not "Roger."

The great majority of ATC transmissions should be answered with Wilco which means "I understand and will comply":

> TOWER **"Piper 70497, follow the Piper on downwind"**

> PILOT **"Wilco, 497"**

> TOWER **"Piper 70497, contact Seattle Approach Control on 119.2"**

> PILOT **"119.2, Wilco, 497"**

> TOWER **"Piper 70497, taxi into position and hold"**

> PILOT **"Wilco, 497"**

There is one situation in which Wilco won't do the job. If you are directed to hold short of a runway you must confirm that instruction by repeating the directive:

> PILOT **"70497 holding short of runway 21."**

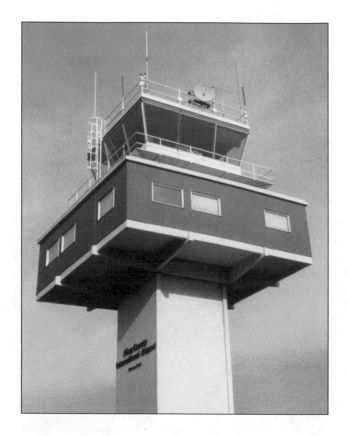

A controller at Chicago O'Hare tells a story about a pilot who called for permission to cross runway 14. "Hold short," was the reply. The pilot immediately added power and taxied across the active runway. "Why did you cross the runway?" he asked the errant pilot. "I asked for permission and you said 'Oh, sure'…" the pilot replied.

Did you notice that whenever I give an example of a reply I put the callsign last? The AIM says that the callsign should be first, so why do I recommend the opposite? Because the controllers prefer that you transmit your callsign last.

Denny Cunningham, a tower controller at O'Hare Airport in Chicago, the world's busiest airport 51 weeks out of the year (Wittman Field in Oshkosh, Wisconsin, gets that honor during the week of the Experimental Aircraft Association's annual fly-in), frequently addresses pilot groups on communications subjects. He says that although two pilots might key their microphones at the same time, it is unlikely that they will both finish talking at the same time. With the callsign transmitted last, ATC is in a better position to clear up misunderstandings.

Other Required Readbacks

Although you will seldom receive vectors or altitude changes from ATC while operating in VFR conditions (this will most likely happen in Class B airspace or when being vectored in Class C airspace), changes in heading or altitude should be read back:

> CONTROLLER **"Piper 70497, climb and maintain 4,000"**
>
> PILOT **"Leaving 2,000 climbing 4,000, 497."**
>
> CONTROLLER **"Piper 70497, turn right heading 330"**
>
> PILOT **"Right 330, 497."**

You should acknowledge transmissions from ATC if for no better reason than to let the controller know that you received the transmissions. At very busy airports, however, the tower controller may be giving instructions to several airplanes at once without pausing for breath. You know that you will cause interference if you key your microphone while the controller is still transmitting, so what do you do? The answer has to be to do nothing. Follow the instructions that apply to your flight without acknowledgment.

"Say Again?"

When in doubt, never hesitate to say "Say again?" It is far better to eliminate any doubt than to take action on what you think you were directed to do, and it is easier on the controller's nerves as well.

Similar Callsigns

Although it happens infrequently, you may find yourself flying in the same patch of air as another airplane with a similar callsign. This can be more than an inconvenience if the pilot of one airplane acknowledges or follows instructions meant for the other pilot. Controllers are pretty sharp at picking up on this possibility and will warn both pilots:

> CONTROLLER **"Piper 234D, be aware that Piper 334D is on the frequency."**

However, you should not rely on the controller but should be alert to the possibility of confusion if you hear an airplane on the frequency with a callsign close to yours.

Don't hesitate to speak up if you hear an error on the frequency. You may cause some embarrassment, but that is better than bent metal:

PILOT "Center, Piper 70497 — I believe that Piper 1234G acknowledged the heading change you gave Piper 1334G."

Controllers are human — they don't catch all of the readback errors.

Another line of defense is situational awareness — if you think that an ATC instruction is addressed to you but it doesn't make sense, speak up. If you are flying Piper 234D and have just reported to the tower that you are five miles out on the 45, an instruction to Piper 234D to "turn base and follow the Baron on final" is obviously not directed to you. You can handle this by saying either "Was that for Piper 234D?" or "Piper 234D is still on the 45."

Type Confusion

Controllers occasionally confuse airplane types, and you must be ready to politely correct the controller when this happens. Controllers make traffic flow decisions based on the performance of the model they think you are flying (they have a quick reference sheet with models and speeds). If you are flying Arrow 369OJ and the controller keeps calling you Cessna 369OJ, it is your responsibility to get the situation straightened out. Plain language works best:

PILOT "Tampa Approach, 369OJ is a Piper Arrow, not a Cessna."

Bear in mind that aircraft registration numbers are unique — the same numbers cannot be assigned to two different aircraft even if they are different models or types. We like to keep airborne communications brief and to the point, but if you don't make it clear to the controller just what kind of airplane you are flying, you are not doing your part:

PILOT "Atlanta Center, 8452B is a *single-engine* Aero Commander."

You should not use the prefix "November" as part of your initial call to an ATC facility. The tail numbers of all U.S.-registered airplanes begin with N, so when you say November you are not telling the controller anything useful.

You should use your full callsign when making the initial call to a station:

PILOT "Norwood Tower, Piper 70497 six miles east for landing with Oscar."

Once communications have been established, you are allowed to use the last three letters or digits. Whenever there is a possibility of confusion with another airplane, use the full callsign preceded by the aircraft type. Confusion breeds disaster.

As you monitor aviation frequencies, you may hear some unfamiliar identifications. **Lifeguard**, followed by an aircraft identification, indicates an air ambulance or emergency helicopter. You should give this airplane's communications priority over yours (it will get priority handling by ATC anyway). **Tango**, used after an aircraft identification, is supposed to be used by air taxi operators. Very few do so, but you may hear it on occasion. An FAA flight test airplane will identify itself as **Flight Test**, and this is a signal for a high level of caution on your part — they fly as low as 50 feet above the runway and frequently fly in the face of normal traffic. If you hear **Air Force One** (or **AF Two**), don't be surprised if area airports are closed for awhile. The Secret Service likes to sterilize the airspace when the President or Vice President are in the area. **Experimental** could mean anything from a KitFox to a Bede jet; keep your eyes open because you can't make any assumptions.

Don't forget the words **Unable** and **Unfamiliar** when communicating with ATC. They are the words to use when you are asked to do something unsafe, or when you are in an area where you are a stranger.

Communicating an Emergency

The emergency VHF frequency is 121.5 MHz, and if you have a problem and don't have time to look up a Center frequency you should switch to 121.5. Following international procedures, the AIM says that if you are in an urgency situation, rather than a distress situation, you should start your transmission on the emergency frequency by saying "Pan, Pan, Pan," followed by your airplane's identification. An urgency situation might be disorientation, while a distress might be empty fuel tanks. In over thirty years of flying I have never heard anyone say "Pan, Pan, Pan"; I have heard some "Mayday" calls, however. Mayday is the internationally accepted word for distress, and it gets the attention of everyone on the frequency. Switch to 121.5 and say:

PILOT **"Mayday, Mayday, Mayday, Piper 40497 calling any station."**

That should result in more than one reply — choose the strongest signal and report your situation to that facility.

Even though you are not talking on or monitoring any ATC frequencies, your transponder should be ON and set to 1200, the VFR code, at all times. The transponder return from your airplane will show up on the controller's scope as an anonymous "1200 squawk"; the controller will have no idea of who you are or at what altitude you are flying, but when you switch to 7700 your return will get immediate attention. ATC records and stores the information displayed on radar scopes, and even if you don't say a word to anyone or squawk 7700 it is possible for them to track your 1200 squawk until it disappears. By the time this takes place, however, you will have been missing for several hours and your survival skills will have been put to the test. This is nice information to know, but you have so many communication options available that your survival should never depend on this procedure. If you think you are lost or if the engine is making funny noises, tell someone about it right away.

If you are receiving radar flight following service and the controller asks you to intensify your transponder return by pushing the "ident" button, accompany that action with a verbal confirmation:

PILOT **"Cessna 1357X, ident."**

Many instructors counsel against this, reasoning that the change in your return on the controller's scope is confirmation enough. Ask any controller about this, however, and you will be told that because of the rate at which the radar sweeps and the screen is refreshed, it may take a couple of sweeps before your enhanced return is seen. In the meantime, the controller has asked you to do something and cannot be sure that you received the transmission. So, speak up.

Simplex vs. Duplex

Aviation communications can be characterized as either simplex or duplex. When you and the controller transmit and receive on the same frequency, which is the usual situation, it is a simplex channel. Put simply, you could not both speak at once and be able to hear one another. There are a few remaining situations in which you will use duplex, where you transmit to ATC on one frequency and listen on another. The most common duplex situation has you transmitting on 122.1 MHz and listening on a VOR frequency; the controller listens to you on 122.1 and transmits on the VOR frequency.

Duplex is being phased out across the country but still exists in some locations. If you look at a VOR frequency box on a sectional chart and see "122.1R" printed above the box it means that a Flight Service Station specialist is listening to a speaker connected to a receiver tuned to 122.1 MHz and will hear your call. That specialist has just one microphone and a selector switch that permits the mike to be connected to one of the many VORs or Remote Communication Outlets in that FSS's area.

When a call is received, a light blinks on the specialists panel if the calling pilot is flying at an altitude that allows reception at only one remote receiver site. If the pilot is flying at an altitude high enough so that the signal reaches two receivers on the same frequency, two lights blink and the specialist has to guess which remote transmitter to use when replying. The solution is simple — a pilot using duplex should always include the name of the VOR in the transmission:

PILOT "**Macon Radio, Baron 1014W, listening to the Dublin VOR.**"

The practice of including the name of the VOR in your initial call is equally applicable to the Enroute Flight Advisory Service, or Flight Watch. When calling for weather information on 122.0 MHz, say:

PILOT "**Gainesville Flight Watch, Piper 70497, over the Jacksonville VOR.**"

I Love A Mystery

Let's say that you are calling Cedar City Flight Watch to check the weather at your destination:

PILOT "**Cedar City Flight Watch, Baron 1014W over Malad,**"

and the response is:

FLIGHT WATCH "**Aircraft over Malad, say again callsign.**"

This simply means that the Flight Watch specialist was busy doing something else and did not catch your callsign. Just provide the information and go on with your request — communications have been established:

PILOT "**Cedar City, Baron 1014W over Malad, request current Rock Springs Weather.**"

A variation of the same scenario is:

FLIGHT WATCH "**Aircraft calling Cedar City Flight Watch, say again callsign.**"

Your transmission has been heard by the ground station, but the specialist is not sure that he or she has logged the callsign correctly.

Hooked On Phonics

Use the phonetic alphabet as published in the *Aeronautical Information Manual*. It may bring a smile to the faces of pilots on the frequency when they hear ATIS information Whiskey referred to as the "Booze News," or King Air 76MM calling in as "76 Mickey Mouse," but it sets a poor example for students and is incomprehensible to pilots for whom English is a second language. The ICAO phonetic alphabet was developed so that pilots from all nations could understand one another.

Also, communicating numbers with accuracy is critically important in aviation. The AIM tells you how to pronounce individual digits to avoid confusion. "Five" and "nine" are the digits most frequently misinterpreted, and you will soon be saying "niner" like a pro.

The AIM tells you to say "four thousand, five hundred" for 4,500. You will hear many pilots at all levels in the aviation industry say "four point five" when reporting that altitude. I cannot argue with doing it the AIM way, but I have no problem with using the decimal notation because in my opinion it is not confusing to either the controller or other pilots on the frequency.

A recent change to the Air Traffic Control Manual has created the best of both worlds: Controllers can now say,

> CONTROLLER **"Baron 1014W, descend and maintain one-zero-thousand, that's ten thousand."**

To gain the most benefit from this change, pilots should begin this practice.

Character	Morse Code	Telephony	Phonic (Pronunciation)
A	● —	Alpha	(AL-FAH)
B	— ● ● ●	Bravo	(BRAH-VOH)
C	— ● — ●	Charlie	(CHAR-LEE) or (SHAR-LEE)
D	— ● ●	Delta	(DELL-TAH)
E	●	Echo	(ECK-OH)
F	● ● — ●	Foxtrot	(FOKS-TROT)
G	— — ●	Golf	(GOLF)
H	● ● ● ●	Hotel	(HOH-TEL)
I	● ●	India	(IN-DEE-AH)
J	● — — —	Juliett	(JEW-LEE-ETT)
K	— ● —	Kilo	(KEY-LOH)
L	● — ● ●	Lima	(LEE-MAH)
M	— —	Mike	(MIKE)
N	— ●	November	(NO-VEM-BER)
O	— — —	Oscar	(OSS-CAH)
P	● — — ●	Papa	(PAH-PAH)
Q	— — ● —	Quebec	(KEH-BECK)
R	● — ●	Romeo	(ROW-ME-OH)
S	● ● ●	Sierra	(SEE-AIR-RAH)
T	—	Tango	(TANG-GO)
U	● ● —	Uniform	(YOU-NEE-FORM) or (OO-NEE-FORM)
V	● ● ● —	Victor	(VIK-TAH)
W	● — —	Whiskey	(WISS-KEY)
X	— ● ● —	Xray	(ECKS-RAY)
Y	— ● — —	Yankee	(YANG-KEY)
Z	— — ● ●	Zulu	(ZOO-LOO)
1	● — — — —	One	(WUN)
2	● ● — — —	Two	(TOO)
3	● ● ● — —	Three	(TREE)
4	● ● ● ● —	Four	(FOW-ER)
5	● ● ● ● ●	Five	(FIFE)
6	— ● ● ● ●	Six	(SIX)
7	— — ● ● ●	Seven	(SEV-EN)
8	— — — ● ●	Eight	(AIT)
9	— — — — ●	Nine	(NIN-ER)
0	— — — — —	Zero	(ZEE-RO)

Figure 3-1. AIM: telephony and ICAO phonetic alphabet

4 Class G Airspace

There's Not Much Of It

According to the most recent statistics, there are about 17,000 airports in the United States and less than 700 of them have control towers. That's why our discussion of communications will literally start at the grassroots level and work toward the complex airspace at busy airports with airline traffic. Although I will refer to and illustrate actual airports, you should understand that whatever works in these situations will apply to any similar airport.

With very few exceptions, Class G airspace exists from ground level up to either 700 feet or 1,200 feet above the ground. There are a few locations (in the western United States) where it extends all the way to 14,500 feet, but for the purposes of this text I am going to ignore them.

Figure 4-1 is an aerial view of the Sky Harbor airport in Sultan, Washington (Airport A on the four-color sectional chart foldout at the back of the book). It is a typical small airport with a couple of rows of hangars and direct access to the turf runway. According to the sectional, no services are available because the airport symbol doesn't have little protrusions sticking out of it. The fact that the symbol is not solid ◯ magenta indicates that the runway surface is not paved.

Your sectional is speckled with similar airport symbols; some have an R for private or non-public airports. These are all perfectly good airports whose owners have removed them from public use status due to liability concerns.

Figure 4-1. Sky Harbor Airport, Sultan, Washington

Sky Harbor does not have magenta tint surrounding it, and the boundary of airspace with a 700-foot AGL floor is just west of the airport, so you must assume that it lies in Class G airspace and that the floor of the overlying Class E airspace is at 1,200 feet AGL. You can taxi out and take off from an airport like Sky Harbor without saying a word to anyone, although the airport does have a UNICOM station as indicated by the frequency 122.8, and the letter C in a magenta oval meaning that 122.8 is the Common Traffic Advisory Frequency (CTAF). It is around airports like Sky Harbor that most airplanes without radios or electrical systems (NORDO—"no radio") can be found.

Does this mean that you should not use your radio if you have one? No way. Use your radio as a tool to increase the safety of flight by staying alert to the positions and intentions of other radio-equipped planes, while keeping a wary eye out for NORDOs.

Excerpt from Callback Newsletter

"I crossed the airport at 1,800 MSL to check the segmented circle for wind and traffic pattern indicators…the pattern indicators indicated runway 19 has a right-hand traffic pattern. I broadcast on 122.9 MHz entering downwind and turning base. Almost immediately thereafter I saw aircraft B coming at me at the same altitude. I turned right, broadcasting that I was going around and aircraft B turned left, landing on runway 19. At no time did the pilot of aircraft B announce his intentions…."

UNICOM and MULTICOM

A UNICOM is a ground station purchased by the airport operator, licensed by the FCC, and operated by employees of the FBO. A UNICOM has no official standing whatsoever. The Aeronautical Information Manual says that a UNICOM is an "Aeronautical Advisory Station," whereas a Flight Service Station is an "Airport Advisory Station." Although UNICOM and MULTICOM look like acronyms, the letters do not mean anything.

Any information you receive from a UNICOM is wholly advisory in nature and should be supplemented by your own observations. If the UNICOM operator says that there is no traffic in the pattern and you almost get T-boned on downwind, that is not the fault of the UNICOM operator. If the UNICOM operator says that runway 9 is in use and you want to take off on runway 27, have at it (but you will probably get some heat from other pilots in the area who are on the frequency).

The most common use of the UNICOM frequency is obtaining information on the runway in use. However, you can use it to ask the operator to call a taxi, to call someone and advise of your estimated time of arrival, to ask for a quick turnaround from the fuelers, to request two hamburgers, one with onions, one without, and two chocolate milkshakes be ready when you land. In other words, it is good for just about anything within reason except official weather reports or takeoff and landing clearances.

MULTICOM, 122.9 MHz, is the Common Traffic Advisory Frequency at airports that have no UNICOM. Accordingly, when you use 122.9, your transmissions are to other airplanes in flight and not to anyone on the ground.

Let's Go Bore Some Holes in the Sky

Having said all that, let's take off from Sky Harbor. It is like the majority of small airports in having only one runway and a broad area that leads from the ramp/tie-down area to the runway, although the path from the ramp to the runway is usually better defined. There is no taxiway paralleling the runway. This means that departing airplanes must taxi in the face of arriving traffic to get to the runup position (back-taxiing), and that pilots who roll past the midfield exit must do a 180 and taxi back to the exit.

As noted before, Sky Harbor's Common Traffic Advisory Frequency is 122.8 MHz; other UNICOM frequencies are 122.7 and 123.0, with some others being reserved by the Federal Communication Commission for UNICOM assignment when necessary. If Sky Harbor had no ground radio station at all, the CTAF would be 122.9, which is the MULTICOM frequency.

While still on the taxiway at Sky Harbor before entering the runway, you transmit on 122.8 MHz, saying:

> PILOT **"Sky Harbor traffic, Piper 70497 back-taxiing for takeoff on runway 27, Sky Harbor."**

Why don't you address your transmission to Sky Harbor UNICOM? Because your intentions to back-taxi are of no interest to the person in the airport office, only to the pilots operating in the vicinity of the airport.

Before you actually taxi onto the runway, it is a good idea to do a 360-degree turn, or maneuver as necessary, to see the final approach from both directions and to check for airplanes on base as well. Sky Harbor has no pattern direction markings, according to the photograph, so a standard left-hand traffic pattern is in effect. (*See* Figure 4-2.)

Single Runway

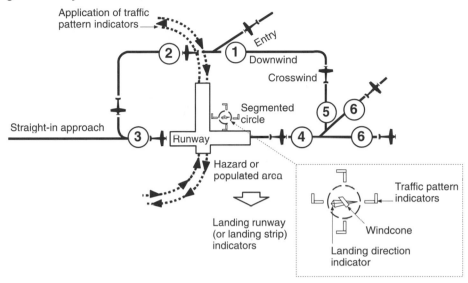

Figure 4-2. Traffic pattern, single runway (from AC90-66A)

When you are checking for airplanes on base leg, however, don't forget that all pilots are not as smart as you are and someone might very well be on right base. And don't forget about the NORDO (no radio) airplanes that couldn't hear your announcement in the first place.

While taxiing east toward the runup area for runway 27, monitor 122.8 so that if someone makes an announcement about entering the pattern (or worse, reports 3 miles out on final) you can repeat that you are back-taxiing and will clear the runway at the end.

Most airports of this type have provided a wide spot at each end of the runway so that pilots can perform their pretakeoff checks clear of the runway surface. If this is not the case at an airport you are using, complete your runup on the taxiway or ramp before taxiing onto the runway (use good etiquette — turn so that your propwash won't affect airplanes taxiing behind you).

If you are of a slow and methodical nature — and that's better than being rash and impetuous — then perform as much of the runup as possible before you even enter the taxiway, wherever one exists. This also applies to instructional flights where the instructor explains at great length every detail of the runup procedure. In other words, don't block the taxiway any longer than absolutely necessary.

When you have completed your pretakeoff preparations and are ready to go, take a good long look at the base legs and final approach again and then transmit:

> PILOT **"Piper 70497 departing Sky Harbor runway 27, standard departure" [or "straight-out," or "climbing," or "downwind departure"].**

Either "staying in the pattern" or "closed traffic" is appropriate if you are just going to practice takeoffs and landings at Sky Harbor. In that situation, saying,

> PILOT **"Piper 70497 is staying in the pattern at Sky Harbor"**

— serves to advise everyone in the area who is monitoring the frequency.

The idea is to give approaching pilots some insight into where you are going so that they can avoid you.

For the purpose of this exercise, however, you are going to fly about 13 miles to Harvey Field in Snohomish (Airport B on the sectional chart excerpt) for one of those $100 hamburgers that pilots enjoy so much. If you remain less than 1,200 feet above the ground until you reach the edge of the magenta tint (see the glider symbol?), then duck down to less than 700 feet above the ground, you will stay in Class G airspace. During daylight hours, you will need to avoid touching a cloud with any portion of your airplane and have one mile flight visibility, if you are to fly legally under basic visual flight rules. Flying in those conditions is not the smartest thing to do, however, because you will be bending (if not breaking) the minimum altitude rules, and the hamburger almost certainly will not be worth the risk of violating the Federal Aviation Regulations.

To add a little fun to the trip, your buddy Joe is going to fly his Bellanca to Harvey Field (Figure 4-3) so that you can commiserate about the cost of hamburgers (and annual inspections). After you have both departed from Sky Harbor you can get together on the plane-to-plane frequency, 122.75 MHz, and chat about the scenery. This frequency and 122.85 are the only frequencies approved for fixed-wing chatter between airborne pilots, according to the AIM.

Figure 4-3. Harvey Field, Snohomish, Washington

By the way, if someone tells you that 123.45 MHz is an acceptable plane-to-plane frequency, keep one hand on your money. The Federal Communications Commission guards its frequency assignment duties jealously and will fine pilots who misuse their radios. Out here in the Pacific Northwest, 123.45 MHz is assigned to the Boeing Company for flight-test purposes; someone else probably has been assigned that frequency in your area. You can be sure that it has not been allocated to anyone for plane-to-plane communication.

You Want Fries With That?

The airport symbol for Harvey Field is solid magenta and shows one runway, which means that it has a hard-surfaced runway more than 1,500 feet long, and it has the little protrusions that mean "services" to the mapmakers and "fuel" to pilots; CTAF is 123.0 MHz. Before you leave the Harvey Field area on the sectional chart excerpt, note the parachute symbol just west of the field. It might be a good idea to check in with the UNICOM and check on jumping activity:

> PILOT "Harvey UNICOM, Piper 70497 ten miles east, landing Harvey. Could you give me the runway in use and advise of any parachuting activity?"

> UNICOM "Piper 70497, Harvey UNICOM, runway 32 is in use, two aircraft in the pattern, no jump activity."

> PILOT "70497, understand runway 32."

Note from Figure 4-3 that there is a pattern indicator with a tetrahedron just east of runway 32 (northeast of the grove of trees). It is indicating that the traffic pattern is to the west; that is, left traffic for runway 32 and right traffic for runway 14. This type of restriction is common when the local municipality wants to keep airplanes from flying over the city. At Harvey Field, the downwind leg is flown over the fields west of the airport no matter which way the wind is blowing.

If you are a fairly inexperienced pilot who is being trained at a tower-controlled airport, you must understand that UNICOM is diametrically opposite from tower control. The UNICOM transmitter/receiver is supposed to be on during operating hours, but that doesn't mean that there is someone standing close by just waiting for your call. The UNICOM operator might be out on the ramp pumping gas, calling a motel for transportation, or just out of the office for a few minutes. In other words, you should not be surprised if you call UNICOM and fail to get a reply.

Switch to the UNICOM frequency about 10 miles out. Devote a few minutes to just "reading the mail" (that's ham operator talk for "just listening in"). Chances are that you will hear other airplanes in the Harvey Field area getting runway information from the UNICOM operator and you can use that information to plan your approach to the pattern. If you hear,

> PILOT "Harvey UNICOM, Piper 70497, airport advisory."

> UNICOM "Piper 70497, Harvey UNICOM, Runway 32 is the active; there are three in the pattern"

— you have the information you need to plan an entry to the traffic pattern. If there isn't anyone on the frequency who is flying near Harvey you will probably hear transmissions from pilots flying near other airports that share 123.0 MHz with

Harvey Field. The UNICOM frequencies can become really crowded on a nice day, and you have to listen closely to pick out the transmissions that apply to your destination airport.

The Aeronautical Information Manual suggests that pilots "self-announce," their position when about 10 miles from the destination airport, giving their identification, position in relation to the airport, altitude, and intentions:

> PILOT **"Harvey traffic, Piper 70497 10 miles east, two thousand five hundred feet, landing [or 'touch and go'] Harvey."**

It is important to mention the name of the airport at both the beginning and end of each self-announced transmission so that pilots monitoring the frequency will know at which airport you are operating.

The Tower of Babble

The AIM also suggests that pilots operating at non-tower airports make self-announced reports on downwind, base, final and when exiting the runway:

> PILOT **"Harvey traffic, Piper 70497 entering downwind, Harvey.**

> PILOT **"Harvey traffic, Piper 70497 turning left base, Harvey"**

> PILOT **"Harvey traffic, Piper 70497 on final, touch and go, Harvey."**

> PILOT **"Harvey traffic, Piper 70497, clear of the active."**

A little bit of common sense helps a lot in this situation. I yield to no one in my respect for the regulations and approved procedures, but if every pilot made every report suggested by the AIM at every small airport on a sunny weekend afternoon the UNICOM frequencies would be saturated. After a few minutes in the traffic pattern you will have a handle on just how much activity there is and how necessary it is for you to make transmissions that no one is listening to. Certainly, if there are four airplanes in the touch-and-go pattern and itinerant airplanes are coming in to make full-stop landings, safety dictates position and intention reports. On the other hand, if you have the pattern to yourself you might want to reconsider making *every* report suggested by the AIM.

By the way, your airplane will be more visible to other pilots when its wings are banked, so I like "turning downwind," "turning base," "turning final," instead of reporting when established on one of those legs of the pattern.

Did you notice that nothing has been said about filing a flight plan or asking for radar flight following? Those are both excellent ways to cut down search time if you have a problem and must make an emergency landing.

When is a Tower Not a Tower?

Is the airspace around an airport with a tower ever Class G airspace? Can you tell by looking at the sectional chart? The answers are yes and no. When the last controller turns off the lights and locks the door, we know that Class D airspace will not exist at that airport until the early bird controller shows up in the morning. But in the meantime, is the airspace Class E or Class G? The only place you will find the answer to that question is the Airport/Facility Directory.

If there will be a weather observer there all night, then it is Class E airspace all the way to the ground and you must get a Special VFR clearance if you want to depart in weather that is less than VFR. (If you are not instrument rated, you can't legally ask for an SVFR clearance at night.) One mile visibility and clear of clouds is necessary to operate in Class E surface area — three miles visibility is required at night.

If no weather observer will be present, then the airspace from field elevation to 700 feet above the ground becomes Class G airspace.

On the sectional chart excerpt, note the Olympia airport (C) and the Tacoma Narrows Airport (D). Both have part-time towers, as indicated by the asterisk next to the tower frequency. Both are surrounded by blue dashed lines, indicating the horizontal dimensions of the tower's class D airspace when the tower is in operation. Now look at Figure 4-4, containing a portion of the Airport/Facility Directory listing for both airports: Olympia's airspace becomes Class E when the controller goes home, but because Tacoma Narrows has no full-time weather observer, its airspace becomes Class G when the controller goes home. You just can't rely on the sectional chart to tell you everything you need to know.

A magenta halo around an airport symbol has special meaning to VFR pilots. That magenta circle means that the floor of controlled airspace (Class E) dips to 700 feet above the ground and, not coincidentally, that the airport has at least one instrument approach procedure. Note the subtle trap — go up from the surface 699 feet and you remain in Class G airspace with its daytime rule of "clear of clouds." You can fool around (and I use the phrase advisedly) beneath the clouds doing touch-and-goes with a mere mile of flight visibility. Gain one more foot of altitude and you are in Class E airspace, honor bound to stay 500 feet below, 1,000 feet above, and 2,000 feet laterally from all clouds with three miles visibility. Why? Because a pilot flying on instruments can pop out of one of those clouds and surprise you. Ellensburg, Airport E on the sectional chart (and Figure 4-5), is an example.

TACOMA NARROWS (TIW)   4 W   UTC –8(–7DT)   N47°16.08' W122°34.69'   **SEATTLE**
    292   B   S4   **FUEL** 80, 100, 100LL, JET A   OX 4   TPA—1300(1008)   LRA   **H–1A, L–1D**
    RWY 17-35: H5002X150 (ASPH–AFSC)   S–50, D–80, DT–80   MIRL   **IAP**
      RWY 17: MALSR. PAPI(P4L)—GA 3.0°. TCH 50'. Trees. Rgt. tfc.   **RWY 35:** REIL. VASI(V4L)—GA 3.0° TCH 51'.
    AIRPORT REMARKS: Attended 1600–0400Z‡. Deer on and in vicinity of arpt. Noise sensitive arpt, for noise abatement
      and tfc procedures call arpt manager 206–591–5759 or 206–851–3544. Rwy 35 REIL out of svc indefinitely.
      ACTIVATE MALSR Rwy 17 and PAPI Rwy 17—CTAF. Landing fee acft over 12,500 lbs.
    WEATHER DATA SOURCES: LAWRS
    COMMUNICATIONS: CTAF 118.5   **ATIS** 124.05 (1600–0400Z‡)   **UNICOM** 122.95
      SEATTLE FSS (SEA) TF 1–800–WX–BRIEF. NOTAM FILE TIW.
    ® **SEATTLE APP/DEP CON** 120.1
      TOWER 118.5 (1600–0400Z‡)   **GND CON** 121.8
  → **AIRSPACE: CLASS D** svc effective 1600–0400Z‡ other times CLASS G.
    RADIO AIDS TO NAVIGATION: NOTAM FILE TCM.
      McCHORD (T) VORTAC 109.6   TCM   Chan 33   N47°08.86' W122°28.50'   308° 8.4 NM to fld. 285/22E.
      GRAYE NDB (MHW/LOM) 216   GR   N47°09.02' W122°36.29'   349° 7.2 NM to fld. NOTAM FILE GRF.
      ILS 109.1   I–TIW   Rwy 17   ILS unmonitored when twr clsd.
    COMM/NAVAID REMARKS: Emerg frequency 121.5 not avbl at twr.

OLYMPIA

   AERO PLAZA (WA44)   5 SE   UTC –8(–7DT)   N46°59.56' W122°49.66'   **SEATTLE**
    213
    RWY 07-25: 2015X116 (TURF)
      RWY 07: Trees.   **RWY 25:** Trees.
    AIRPORT REMARKS: Unattended.
    COMMUNICATIONS: CTAF 122.9
      SEATTLE FSS (SEA) TF 1–800–WX–BRIEF. NOTAM FILE SEA.

OLYMPIA (OLM)   4 S   UTC –8(–7DT)   N46°58.24' W122°54.17'   **SEATTLE**
    206   B   S4   **FUEL** 80, 100, 100LL, JET A   OX 1, 2   LRA   ARFF Index Ltd   **H–1A, L–1C**
    RWY 17-35: H5419X150 (ASPH)   S–55, D–69, DT–117   MIRL   **IAP**
      RWY 17: MALSR. Thld dsplcd 427'. Road.   **RWY 35:** VASI(V4L)—GA 3.0° TCH 50'. Trees. Rgt tfc.
    RWY 08-26: H5001X150 (ASPH)   S–30
      RWY 08: Ground. Rgt tfc.   **RWY 26:** Tree.
    AIRPORT REMARKS: Attended Apr–Sep 1600Z‡–sunset. For svc after hours call 206–754–4043 or 206–786–8333.
      Coyotes on and in vicinity of rwys. PPR for unscheduled air carrier ops with more than 30 passenger seats call
      arpt manager 206–586–6164. Rwy 08–26 and Taxiways F, G, C, E and D not avbl for air carrier ops with more
      than 30 passenger seats. NSTD hold short lgts intersection Twy E and Rwy 17. During hours twr clsd ACTIVATE
      MALSR Rwy 17 and VASI Rwy 35—CTAF. NOTE: See SPECIAL NOTICE—Land and Hold Short Operations.
    COMMUNICATIONS: CTAF 124.4   **UNICOM** 122.95
      SEATTLE FSS (SEA) TF 1–800–WX–BRIEF. NOTAM FILE OLM.
    ® **SEATTLE APP/DEP CON** 121.1
      TOWER 124.4 (1600–0400Z‡)   **GND CON** 121.6
  → **AIRSPACE: CLASS D** svc effective 1600–0400Z‡ other times CLASS E.
    RADIO AIDS TO NAVIGATION: NOTAM FILE OLM.
      (H) VORTACW 113.4   OLM   Chan 81   N46°58.30' W122°54.11'   at fld. 200/19E.
      VOR portion unusable:

043°–082° blo 17,500'	333°–358° byd 25 NM blo 6,000'
143°–183° byd 20 NM blo 6,000'	358°–043° byd 10 NM blo 6,000'
333°–358° byd 10 NM blo 4,000'	358°–043° byd 20 NM blo 7,000'
DME unusable:	
223°–258° byd 20 NM blo 4,100'	358°–043° byd 10 NM blo 6,000'
258°–283° byd 30 NM blo 4,100'	358°–043° byd 20 NM blo 7,000'

      ILS 111.9   I–OLM   Rwy 17   Unmonitored during hours twr closed. BC unusable.
    COMM/NAVAID REMARKS: Emerg frequency 121.5 not avbl at twr.

Figure 4-4. Tacoma Narrows, Olympia, WA — excerpts from A/FD

Figure 4-5. Bowers Field, Ellensburg, Washington

The first rule of operations for VFR pilots at such an airport is to stay on the ground unless the base of the clouds is at least 1,500 feet above the airport. (You have to be 500 feet below the clouds for pattern work, right?) That will give an approaching instrument pilot a clear view of the airport long before the airplane leaves controlled airspace, letting you do your takeoff and landing practice in safety.

The second rule is a little more complicated. If the airport has a UNICOM or no radio at all, you want to be on the appropriate frequency to make your position reports in the pattern and to hear other pilots in the area. At the same time, it would be helpful if you could listen to the appropriate air traffic control frequency to hear any transmissions from inbound pilots who are shooting the instrument approach. Weather has nothing to do with this, by the way — pilots working on their instrument ratings frequently practice approaches in VFR weather while wearing a hood or other view-limiting device.

This is the way it should work: The ATC controller tells the instrument pilot (on the ATC frequency),

CONTROLLER **"Cleared for the approach, change to advisory frequency approved."**

That tells the instrument pilot to switch to UNICOM or MULTICOM to tell pilots like you that they are coming your way and most likely will make a straight-in approach instead of flying a rectangular pattern. Because you have one receiver tuned to the ATC frequency you are ahead of the game— you know what to expect.

An instrument pilot who is not too sharp will switch over to UNICOM or MULTICOM and say something like,

PILOT **"Podunk traffic, Baron 1014W at RIBIT, low approach."**

(RIBIT is an example of a fix or intersection in an instrument approach procedure.) You, of course, being neither an instrument pilot nor in training for the rating, have no idea what RIBIT is. It gives you no clue at all as to what is going on, and probably makes you mad if your instructor has drummed into your head the incorrect information that straight-in approaches are a no-no. Tell your instructor to read Advisory Circular 90-66A (and look back at Figure 4-2).

An instrument pilot or student who is more on the ball might say:

PILOT **"Podunk traffic, Baron 70497 five miles out, straight in on an instrument approach."**

If you regularly fly into airports with instrument approaches it might be a good idea to get together with your instructor (who is instrument-rated, of course) and talk about how the instrument folks operate in the vicinity of any uncontrolled airports you use frequently.

Excerpt from NASA Report

"I was turning final on 34 (right traffic). Aircraft B was making a straight-in approach. I saw B, made 360-degree turn to avoid collision. Right traffic is normally in effect for this runway. I made calls stating my position on downwind and base on 122.8. Aircraft B pilot later told me he was being vectored by Midland Approach and was not on 122.8 and did not see me until I made an evasive turn."

Summary

As a practical matter, you are not going to spend much time in Class G airspace — it is too close to the ground. The only (dubious) advantage of Class G airspace is the relaxed daytime VFR visibility and cloud clearance requirements. Flying with only one mile visibility and clear of clouds is rightly dubbed "scud running" and doing so has led to many accidents attributed to "inadvertent VFR flight into instrument meteorological conditions." At night, the requirements for VFR flight in Class G airspace are much more stringent.

Still, the communication situations we have discussed are valid and will be found to apply equally well in Class E airspace.

One final anecdote about the use of radios at uncontrolled airports:

Two retired pilots (airline or military or both, I can't remember which) had worked separately for hundreds of hours each restoring antique biplanes. One Sunday morning each of them decided to go flying from an uncontrolled airport in Class G airspace. The windsock was hanging straight down. One taxied to the east end of the runway, the other to the west end — these airplanes are notorious for poor pilot visibility and neither saw the other airplane taxiing. Because of a hump in the center of the runway, neither pilot could see the other as they moved into position for takeoff. When they saw that they were going to collide in the middle of the runway, each veered to the right and there was nothing but torn fabric and broken ribs where the left wings used to be.

Both airplanes had radios, but neither pilot had said a word because "at an uncontrolled field you don't have to use your radio." I'm sure both pilots reconsidered that logic as they totaled up the damage.

⑤ Class E Airspace

It's Your Typical Flight Environment

A flight from one small airport to another, at the relatively low altitudes of Class G airspace, places few communications demands on you. Checking in with the air traffic control system is usually a waste of time because their radar coverage is minimal to nonexistent close to the ground. Tree-top flying in light airplanes (and I mean the really light ones, like ultralight airplanes) is fun and won't result in a lot of noise complaints if the flights take place away from population centers. However, serious cross-country flying means getting into Class E airspace.

Because Class E airspace exists from 700 feet AGL or 1,200 feet all the way to 18,000 feet MSL, there is a tremendous volume of it in the United States and you will spend most of your flying hours buzzing around in it. When you crossed the magenta tint line between Sky Harbor and Harvey Field, the floor of Class E airspace dropped from 1,200 feet to 700 feet above the ground. Unless you were flying low enough to have people report you to the FAA for unwarranted low flying, you entered Class E airspace at that moment.

We've flown from Sky Harbor to Harvey Field and have used plane-to-plane and UNICOM frequencies. Your friend Joe is going back to Sky Harbor. It's time to stretch your wings and fly cross-country from Harvey Field to Olympia (Figure 5-1, and Airport C on the sectional chart), about 65 miles away. The smart thing for you to do now is to go into the pilot lounge to prepare a flight plan and file it by telephone. Even if Harvey Field had a Remote Communications Outlet, filing on the radio when a phone is available is poor practice. Dialing 1-800-WX-BRIEF will do the trick no matter where you are.

It's too early in the book to get involved with Class B or D airspace, so your flight to Olympia will be via airways: direct to the Paine Field VOR, then V-287 to OLM. With the exercise of a little imagination and application of the FARs, you will be able to remain in Class E airspace all the way to the Olympia area.

Departing Harvey Field

Harvey Field has a paved runway (and a grass runway) with a taxiway leading from the gas island to the runup area. You could fire up your radio after starting the engine and call the UNICOM operator to learn which runway is in use, but haven't you had an opportunity to check the windsock and to monitor landing and departing traffic while preflighting your airplane? If that hasn't been the case (your airplane might be in between two rows of hangars) you could taxi out to a position with a direct line-of-sight to the FBO office and say:

PILOT "**Harvey UNICOM, Piper 70497, request runway in use**" [or, "**what is the active?**"]

At locations with parachuting activity, such as Harvey, it might be a good idea to ask the UNICOM operator about any planned jump activity; the situation may have changed since you arrived.

With the runway information in hand, and considering that airplanes might be taxiing out from other tie-down areas or between rows of hangars, it is a good idea to warn others of your intentions by transmitting:

PILOT "**Piper 70497 taxiing from the ramp to runway 32.**"

Many small airports such as Harvey Field have a tetrahedron in addition to one or more windsocks, and it is not unusual for airport management to tie the tetrahedron in position to indicate the preferred runway to a commuter or regional airline flight. Never base your plans on the position of a tetrahedron — go by the windsock (*see* Figure 5-1).

Once you have warned any potentially conflicting ground traffic of your intended taxi route, just keep your eyes open and your finger off of the push-to-talk switch until you have completed your runup and have checked the skies visually for landing traffic. Then,

PILOT "**Harvey traffic, Piper 70497 departing runway 32, [standard, downwind, straight-out] departure**"

— will do the trick. When you are airborne, don't be in a hurry to switch away from the UNICOM frequency; if you are westbound, and an incoming pilot calls Harvey traffic to report five miles west, that is information you want to hear.

Figure 5-1. Runway indicators

Now it is time to open that flight plan you filed on the telephone with the Seattle Flight Service Station:

> PILOT **"Seattle Radio, Piper 70497, 122.55 over."**

(See the FSS frequency above the PAE VOR frequency box?)

> RADIO **"497, Seattle Radio."**

> PILOT **"Seattle Radio, Piper 70497, please open my VFR flight plan from Harvey Field to Olympia via Victor 287 at ten minutes past the hour."**

> RADIO **"497, Seattle Radio, your flight plan is open. Seattle altimeter 30.12. Have a nice flight."**

That exchange is perfectly proper, but you could spend less time on the air by doing it all in one transmission:

PILOT "Seattle Radio, Piper 70497 on 122.55, please open my VFR flight plan from Harvey Field to Olympia at ten minutes past the hour."

The AIM says that the initial callup can be omitted if radio reception is reasonably assured, and at a large Automated Flight Service Station such as Seattle's, with lots of specialists, this would probably work. At a more remote FSS (the kind that are being shut down), the call-up and response method might work better because chances are that the lone specialist is on the phone or otherwise busy.

You have now laid the groundwork for a search effort if you should fail to arrive at Olympia fairly close to your estimated time of arrival. The search-and-rescue folks don't like to be forced to spread their efforts over thousands of square miles of terrain if you do end up missing, and you can help them (and yourself) quite a bit by making position reports. For some reason this is becoming a lost art among pilots, and FSS specialists almost seem surprised when they receive one; but it is a wise practice for you to follow. Looking at the sectional, it would appear that the Apex airport (near Poulsbo on V287) would be a good reporting point. But let's get on our way to Olympia.

Over the Top of Paine Field

You opened your flight plan as soon as you could safely do so after leaving the immediate vicinity of Harvey Field; now, because you have filed a route direct to the Paine Field VOR (Figure 5-2, and Airport F on the sectional), you have a decision to make. When Paine's control tower is in operation (see the asterisk indicating that it is a part-time tower?), Class D airspace is in effect inside that blue dashed line, and Class D airspace doesn't show up until the next chapter!

Just to stay on the subject of this chapter, I suggest that you fly over the Class D airspace to remain in Class E airspace. Paine's field elevation is 606 feet above sea level, and Class D airspace extends 2,500 feet above ground level, so you need to be at least 3,107 feet MSL to clear it. It is only three nautical miles from Harvey Field to the boundary of Paine's Class D airspace, and I doubt that most small planes based at an airport like Sky Harbor can climb 1,000 feet per minute. So just for the purpose of the exercise you will circle up to 3,000 feet over the Snohomish Valley west of Harvey Field, before heading west and climbing to 4,500 feet, the proper altitude for your direction of flight (you don't have to observe the hemispherical rule while climbing or descending).

Figure 5-2. Paine Field, Everett, Washington

What if the base of the clouds was at 2,500 feet? What if you just didn't want to spiral up to 3,000 feet? Would you go around the Class D airspace? I sure hope not. It only takes a moment to say on 120.2 MHz (Paine's control tower frequency):

PILOT **"Paine Tower, Piper 70497, I'd like to cross the field east to west at 2,500 feet."**

TOWER **"Piper 70497, Paine Tower, cleared as requested, report clear."**

When you are over Paine Field you can tune your VOR receiver to 110.6 MHz and put the Omnibearing Selector on 236° for course guidance along V-287.

Now that didn't hurt a bit, did it? As soon as you reach the west side of the dashed blue line, simply say,

PILOT **"Paine Tower, 497 is clear to the west"**

— and go on your way. When the tower is closed, you don't have to talk to anyone because the Class D airspace becomes Class G from the surface up to 700 feet AGL — but you knew that because you looked it up in the Airport/Facility Directory.

Extensions

Notice that Paine Field (and Olympia) have magenta dashed lines abutting the Class D airspace. These indicate Class E extensions, designated to protect instrument flights inbound to the airport. As is the case in other Class E airspace, there is no communication requirement for flight through the extensions. However, regulations or no regulations, it doesn't make good sense to fly silently through an area which you know is used by inbound instrument pilots. If you decide to fly around Class D airspace to avoid talking to the tower, do not fly through a Class E extension. It's just common sense.

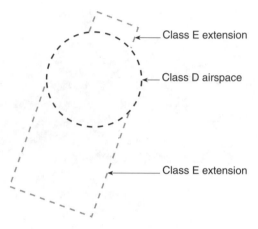

Figure 5-3. Class E extension

Making Position Reports

As your cross-country courseline takes you close to remote communication outlets or airports with Flight Service Stations on the field, just give them a call on the frequency shown on the chart (remember to include the frequency in your initial call) and, after they have acknowledged your call, say:

PILOT **"Seattle Radio, Piper 70497 on 122.5 [or 123.65*] over Apex at 45 past the hour on a VFR flight plan to Olympia."**

* see the RCO frequency box just southeast of Apex?

The FSS specialist will acknowledge your call and give you the current altimeter setting. At the same time, the specialist will log your call and the time of reception, and if you fail to land at the appointed time, the authorities will know that you got at least as far as Apex.

"With a ceiling of 700 feet, a GA aircraft was practicing pattern work at what he said was 500 feet AGL. I consider it unsafe when we break out right at minimums on the circling approach, switch frequencies from Approach to UNICOM and hear someone say he will do a 360 on crosswind to avoid the jet. We could all have been dead right."

Radar Flight Following

Do you wear both a belt and suspenders? If that is the case, or if you just like to take advantage of the services your tax dollars have purchased, by all means use radar flight following in addition to filing a VFR flight plan. When your flight is being followed by radar, you can forget about making position reports.

Unless you are departing from an airport that has a terminal radar facility — and that would most likely be one in Class B, C, or D airspace — you will make your request for radar flight following to an Air Route Traffic Control Center, called Center for short. You will find Center frequencies in the back of the Airport/Facility Directory or by calling an FSS:

> PILOT **"Seattle Radio, Piper 70497 over Paine Field — what is the Center frequency in this area?"**

> RADIO **"Piper 70497, Seattle Radio, contact Seattle Center on 125.1 in that area."**

> PILOT **"497, 125.1, thank you."**

> PILOT **"Seattle Center, Piper 70497 over Paine Field at 2,500 feet, request flight following."**

> CENTER **"497, Seattle Center, squawk 3456 and ident [pause] radar contact, advise any altitude change."**

When departing from a tower-controlled airport, tell the local controller when you report ready for takeoff:

> PILOT **"Galveston Tower, Baron 1014W is ready for takeoff. Request handoff for radar flight following."**

The local controller will check with the radar folks and, workload permitting, you will get a discrete transponder squawk and hear this after you have taken off:

> TOWER **"Baron 1014W, contact Departure 134.45"**

I suggest that you either buy an IFR low altitude en route chart that covers your area of operations, or ask an instrument-rated friend to give you an expired chart instead of recycling it. Learning to find Center frequencies on low altitude charts will take about two minutes, max. You must understand that the sole duty of air traffic controllers is providing separation between IFR flights. Any service provided to a VFR flight is on a workload-permitting basis, and if the controller's response to your request for flight following is "Unable," you will just have to do without. The controller might be swamped with work or just having a bad hair day — it doesn't make any difference.

Don't panic if you call Approach control and get Departure control; if you are wrong, the controller will give you the correct frequency. This is how that might happen — if the runway being used for instrument departures is 36 and you are arriving from the north, you are in Departure's airspace, aren't you? The ATIS (Automated Terminal Information Service) would give you a clue. But you figure that you are an arrival, so you call Approach. Big deal. The controller has heard it a million times.

Once you are in the system, each Center controller will arrange for the controller in the next sector to pick you up and will then tell you to contact that controller on a new frequency. It will still be Center, but a different frequency and usually (but not always, because of remote radar sites), a different voice. Occasionally, Center will lose radar contact because of your distance or altitude and will say:

CENTER **"Baron 1014W, radar contact lost, squawk VFR, change to advisory frequency approved."**

My recommendation in that situation is this:

PILOT **"Fort Worth Center, Baron 1014W would like to stay on this code and contact the next sector when in range."**

That *might* bring,

CENTER **"Baron 1014W continue present squawk, contact Center on 134.8 in ten miles."**

Of course, it might result in "unable," too.

East of the Mississippi, the heavy traffic and complex airway system makes flight following a sometime-thing. Your chances of receiving this service are greater in the west, but it still breaks down to controller workload, and whether or not the controller feels that providing radar service to you will adversely impact his or her primary duty to the folks on IFR flight plans.

Strange Field Entry

As you approach any airport you have a responsibility to other pilots in the area to apprise them of your position and your intentions. Listen on the Common Traffic Advisory Frequency (CTAF) for reports from other pilots already in the pattern; you can't go wrong by going along with the flow. In any event, when you are about ten miles from the airport, transmit:

> PILOT "Podunk area traffic, Piper 70497 is ten miles northeast for touch-and-goes at Podunk."

Then make position reports on the 45, downwind, base, and final if you think they are appropriate.

This accomplishes two things: It lets others know that you are going to join the pattern, and it gives them an indication of where to look for you. If you hear someone say something on the frequency that implies a possible conflict, speak up!

> PILOT "Piper 497 is on the 45."

> PILOT "Piper 497, Baron 1014W turning crosswind to downwind does not have you in sight."

Or,

> PILOT "Podunk traffic, Baron 1014W is straight in for runway 19, practice NDB approach."

> PILOT "Baron 1014W, Piper 40497 is on base for 19, has you in sight; we'll be touch-and-go ahead of you."

Departing a Strange Field in Class E Airspace

There is no substitute for advice from the locals. If you are departing, ask one of the instructors (or a fueler, or the person at the counter) if there are any special departure procedures you should be aware of. As an arrival, if you have researched the A/FD there are probably no surprises. However, it is not unusual for an itinerant pilot to scan the airport bulletin board and learn that the local airport authority has an ordinance that he or she violated on the way in.

No Radio (NORDO)

Although it may be hard to believe in this enlightened age, there are airplanes flying around in the friendly skies without radios. The assumption that a quiet frequency means that there is no traffic in the pattern can be quite dangerous. Another form of NORDO is the airplane with an instructor who has turned the radio volume down because it was interfering with his or her comments to the student.

Special Visual Flight Rules

When an airport in Class E airspace has an instrument approach and also has full-time weather observers, Class E airspace begins at the surface; the boundaries of its surface area are shown by dashed lines. Bremerton National Airport (Figure 5-4, and Airport G on the sectional chart) is a good example. Bremerton National does not have a control tower, as indicated by the magenta color of the airport symbol, but the Airport/Facility Directory indicates that Class E airspace is in effect continuously.

A non-instrument-rated pilot (or an instrument-rated pilot who for some reason does not want to file an instrument flight plan), who wants to take off from or land at Bremerton National when the ceiling is less than 1,000 feet or the visibility is less than 3 miles, must receive a Special Visual Flight Rules (SVFR) clearance from ATC. Nothing on the chart indicates that a pilot who wants an SVFR clearance to depart Bremerton has any option other than to file on the telephone by calling 1-800-WX-BRIEF.

A pilot who intends to land at Bremerton and learns that the field is below basic VFR minimums (by listening to the AWOS on 121.2) can either call the Seattle FSS on 122.5/123.65 and request an SVFR clearance; or, call the Seattle Approach/Departure Control radar facility directly on 127.1 MHz. Where did I get that frequency? It sure isn't on the sectional. I know that you will think that I get a royalty from the National Ocean Service for each copy of the Airport/Facility Directory that they sell, but that's the only place a VFR pilot will find that information.

A Special VFR clearance is something new to the average VFR pilot. It contains a transponder code to squawk, and precise directions on how to enter or leave the Class E surface area; and it must be read back to the controller verbatim. Before you ask for an SVFR clearance, have a piece of paper and something to write with at hand.

COMMUNICATIONS: CTAF/UNICOM 122.7
SEATTLE FSS (SEA) TF 1-800-WX-BRIEF. NOTAM FILE PWT.
® SEATTLE APP/DEP CON 127.1
AIRSPACE: CLASS E svc effective continuous.
RADIO AIDS TO NAVIGATION: NOTAM FILE TCM.
McCHORD (T) VORTAC 109.6   TCM   Chan 33   N47°08.86' W122°28.50'

Figure 5-4. Bremerton National Airport, Washington

CONTROLLER "ATC clears Piper 70497 out of the Bremerton National Airport Echo surface area to the east" [note the mountains and the antenna to the west], "maintain Special VFR conditions at or below 1,500 feet until clear. Report clear of the Echo surface area."

Or,

CONTROLLER "ATC clears Piper 70497 into the Bremerton Echo airspace from the north at or below 1,500 feet. Report landing on 127.1."

Beneath the Ceiling

A Special VFR clearance is required in order to operate *beneath the ceiling* while in Class E airspace with weather below basic VFR minimums. If you are flying through Class E airspace on top of a layer of clouds you don't have to say anything to anyone.

Summary

Unless you like to fly at relatively low altitudes, you will do most of your serious cross-country flying in Class E airspace — hopscotching between the other classes of airspace. Pay attention to the visibility and cloud clearance requirements, and set minimums for yourself that are higher than those required by the FARs.

6 Class D Airspace

When is a Tower Not a Tower?

An airport in Class D airspace is shown on a sectional chart with a blue airport symbol; on the sectional chart excerpt there are several: Paine Field, SeaTac, Bocing Field, Renton, Olympia, etc. The Class D airspace extends from the surface to 2,500 feet above airport elevation (in most cases), and its surface area is shown with a blue dashed line. Class D airspace exists *only* when the tower is in operation, however.

Note that I said Class D airspace begins at the surface, not at field elevation. Look at Paine Field, Airport F on the sectional chart. The little "31" in a square indicates that the top of Paine's Class D airspace is 3,100 feet above sea level. But what if you are flying 500 feet above the water just west of Paine — aren't you beneath the Class D airspace because you are lower than field elevation? Absolutely not — Class D airspace starts at the surface, down where all those salmon are, and you must be in communication with the tower even if you are flying below field elevation.

Figure 6-1. Paine Field excerpt from A/FD

The local controller's authority is limited to that cylinder of airspace indicated with blue dashed lines. You must establish two-way radio communication with that controller for authorization to operate within that cylinder. That means, of course, that you must call for authorization well before you reach the dashed line on the chart that marks the boundary. If you are unable to make contact due to a busy frequency, you must circle around outside of the Class D airspace until you do make radio contact. (NORDO operations will be discussed later.)

The shape of the surface area of Class D airspace varies widely, but is always as depicted on sectional charts. To protect inbound IFR flights, the airspace planners create extensions along the inbound courses of instrument approach procedures. Where such an extension is two miles in length or shorter, it is still Class D airspace and you must talk to the tower controller to fly through it. Where an extension is more than two miles in length the excess becomes Class E airspace and you can fly

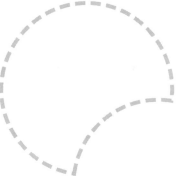

Say Again, Please

through it without talking to the tower — but why would you want to? For that matter, why would you want to fly across the final approach course of an instrument procedure unless you knew for sure that no one was using it?

Class D airspace reverts to Class E or G when the last controller pulls the plug on the coffee pot and goes home. So you have to know the tower's operating hours before you pick up the mike to call for entry into Class D airspace, because you might not need permission. Sectional charts have an asterisk next to the tower frequency when it operates only part-time. The Airport/Facility Directory is a better source of information than any chart, because it gives details on hours of operation and the status of the airspace when the tower is closed (*see* Figure 6-1).

More often than not, Class D airspace becomes Class E all the way to the ground when the tower shuts down, so the visibility and cloud clearance requirements for basic VFR remain in effect. You will have to get a Special VFR clearance from ATC to enter or depart the surface area of the airspace if the ceiling is less than 1,000 feet, or the visibility is less than 3 miles. Notice that the Common Traffic Advisory Frequency is still the tower frequency, even when the tower is closed.

At those airports where the tower controllers are also the weather observers, they take the bottom 700 feet of controlled airspace home with them and leave Class G airspace behind. That means "one mile visibility and clear of clouds" in the daytime and 3 miles visibility with basic VFR cloud clearance at night (except for folks staying within one-half mile of the runway while doing pattern work). Because the airspace is uncontrolled, no SVFR clearance is required if your altitude is less than 700 feet above the ground when within the surface area defined by the blue dashed line.

Two airports that illustrate this point are the Olympia and Tacoma Narrows, Washington, airports (Airports C and D on the sectional chart excerpt). Olympia has a part-time tower but a full-time NWS weather observer. A Special VFR clearance from ATC must be obtained before any operation to, from, or through the Olympia surface area depicted on the sectional (beneath a ceiling of 1,000 feet or less). Tacoma, on the other hand, has no weather capability when the tower is not in operation and during those hours, controlled airspace begins 700 feet above the airport. (I warned you in the Introduction that I would repeat myself when I thought it was important to do so.) You *must* refer to the Airport/Facilities Directory for this information (*see* example in Figure 6-2, next page).

Figure 6-2. Tacoma Narrows Airport, Washington

TACOMA NARROWS (TIW) 4 W UTC – 8(– 7DT) N47°16.08' W122°34.69'   **SEATTLE**
292 B S4 **FUEL** 80, 100, 100LL, JET A OX 4 TPA—1300(1008) LRA   **H–1A, L–1D**
RWY 17-35: H5002X150 (ASPH–AFSC) S–50, D–80, DT–80 MIRL   **IAP**
   RWY 17: MALSR. PAPI(P4L)—GA 3.0°. TCH 50'. Trees. Rgt. tfc.   **RWY 35:** REIL. VASI(V4L)—GA 3.0° TCH 51'.
AIRPORT REMARKS: Attended 1600–0400Z‡. Deer on and in vicinity of arpt. Noise sensitive arpt, for noise abatement
   and tfc procedures call arpt manager 206–591–5759 or 206–851–3544. Rwy 35 REIL out of svc indefinitely.
   ACTIVATE MALSR Rwy 17 and PAPI Rwy 17—CTAF. Landing fee acft over 12,500 lbs.
WEATHER DATA SOURCES: LAWRS
COMMUNICATIONS: CTAF 118.5   **ATIS** 124.05 (1600–0400Z‡)   **UNICOM** 122.95
   SEATTLE FSS (SEA) **TF** 1–800–WX–BRIEF. NOTAM FILE TIW.
Ⓡ **SEATTLE APP/DEP CON** 120.1
   TOWER 118.5 (1600–0400Z‡)   **GND CON** 121.8
AIRSPACE: CLASS D svc effective 1600–0400Z‡ other times CLASS G.
RADIO AIDS TO NAVIGATION: NOTAM FILE TCM.
   McCHORD (T) VORTAC 109.6   TCM   Chan 33   N47°08.86' W122°28.50'   308° 8.4 NM to fld. 285/22E.
   GRAVE NDB (MHW/LOM) 216   GR   N47°09.02' W122°36.29'   349° 7.2 NM to fld. NOTAM FILE GRF.
   ILS 109.1   I–TIW   Rwy 17   ILS unmonitored when twr clsd.
COMM/NAVAID REMARKS: Emerg frequency 121.5 not avbl at twr.

"What's the ATIS?"

Most, but not all, tower-controlled airports provide an Automated Terminal Information Service (ATIS) broadcast either on a discrete frequency (shown on the sectional chart) or a nearby radio navigation aid. The broadcast includes ceiling, visibility, wind, altimeter setting, runway in use, and any special information of importance to pilots.

Under normal conditions, the tower controllers prepare a new tape every time a new weather observation is received, usually every hour. However, if the weather is changing rapidly they will make tapes more frequently.

Each ATIS tape has a phonetic alphabet identifier, and you should use that identifier when making your initial contact with the ground controller when departing, and the tower controller when arriving:

> PILOT **"Boise Ground/Tower, Baron 1014W [give your position and intentions], with information ECHO."**

By doing so, you relieve the controller of the need to give you the current weather observation. Many pilots who have monitored the ATIS will tell the controller that they "have the numbers." ATC will not consider this transmission as assurance that you have received the latest ATIS. Just in case you listened to information ECHO but information FOXTROT is current when you call, it is best to include the phonetic identifier of the ATIS information in your initial transmission.

Listening to the ATIS is a special case of "reading the mail." It will tell you not only which runway is in use but will give you the wind, ceiling, and visibility at the time the tape recording was made, plus other useful information relating to the airport. You can use the ability of your communication receiver to defeat the squelch and get the ATIS information long before you fly into the area.

Tune to the ATIS frequency and turn the squelch knob until static fills your ears and listen for a weak voice signal. It might take a couple of times through the tape before you get everything you want, but by knowing the wind, ceiling, and visibility well

---

ATIS Example:

This is Boeing Field airport information Romeo, 0351Z weather 11,000 scattered, 25,000 thin scattered, visibility 30. Temperature 64, dew point 54. Wind 230 at 5. Altimeter 29.84. ILS runway 13 Right approach, landing departing runways 13 Left and Right. Aircraft landing 13 Left are reminded to fly the VASI. All VFR departures say direction of flight. On initial contact advise you have information Romeo.

---

in advance you have extra planning time. (Some radios may require that you pull on a knob or switch to a "test" position to defeat the squelch.)

At tower-controlled airports that do not provide an ATIS broadcast, the tower controller will give you the ceiling, visibility, wind direction and velocity, and altimeter setting when you make your initial contact. If you have been monitoring the frequency (as you should) and hear this information transmitted to another airplane, you can save the controller a little time and trouble by including "I have the numbers" or "Cessna 1357X has the numbers" when you call. If you are departing from such an airport, the ground controller will do the honors.

Ground Control

The ground controller is usually one of a team of controllers in the tower cab, and ground control is a discrete frequency. Ground control frequencies are almost always 121.7, .8, or .9, so if a controller says "Contact ground point seven" you are expected to know that the frequency is 121.7. If you flip through the Airport/Facilities Directories for several areas, however, you will see that this is not a hard-and-fast rule. You will also learn through experience that during slack times one person serves as both local ("tower") controller and ground controller, so you will either hear the same voice on both frequencies or hear the tower controller say "Taxi to parking."

The ground controller's responsibility is to keep you from running into someone while on a "movement area" of a tower-controlled airport. You can usually, but not always, identify movement areas by a double white line that separates them from the ramp or parking areas. Common sense plays a big role here. If you are in between two lines of T-hangars or in a common tie-down area you are on your own. Don't expect the ground controller to keep you from fender benders until you are ready to enter the taxiway — and don't expect the ground controller to give you any instructions until you are in a movement area. Having the rotating beacon and/or strobes on will help the ground controller find you when you make the initial call, but you should do your part by giving your location as accurately as possible:

> PILOT "Houston Ground Control, Cessna 1357X at the Icarus
> Flight School ramp, VFR to Waco."

> PILOT "Yakima Ground, Baron 1014W at south parking, staying in
> the pattern."

> PILOT "Norfolk Ground, Piper 70497 at the Texaco pumps, taxi
> to the terminal for passenger pickup."

When taxiing for takeoff, stay on the ground control frequency until you are really ready for takeoff. If the plane behind you notices that one of your baggage doors is open, or if the FBO wants you to return to the ramp to pick up the briefcase you left in the pilot lounge, the folks in the tower will attempt to call you on the ground frequency first. If you are the Good Samaritan who is second in line, the drill is,

PILOT "**Ground, Baron 1014W's rear baggage door is open.**"

You aren't supposed to talk directly to another airplane on the ground control frequency, but believe me, the pilot of 14W will get the message.

If the ground controller includes a "hold short" instruction in your taxi clearance you are expected to read it back.

GROUND "**Cessna 1357X, runway 9 taxi, hold short of runway 22.**"

PILOT "**Cessna 1357X is taxiing to runway 9, hold short of 22.**"

Never cross a runway without a clearance; check with the ground controller if you are not sure. Better safe than sorry.

Many airports have parallel runways, and you must understand that the taxiway between the two runways belongs to the tower (local) controller, not the ground controller, when both runways are in use. Instructions to hold short of the parallel runway or to taxi across it to the ramp will come from the tower controller:

TOWER "**Baron 14W, taxi across 13R, contact ground point 9 on the far side.**"

When you are going to a strange airport, nothing beats having some form of airport diagram to help you find your way around on the ground. There are a number of commercial flight guides on sale at your local pilot supply store. Before you walk out to your plane to depart, take a moment to study the airport diagram for your destination. Which side of the airport is the general aviation side? If you have checked the weather at the destination you know what the surface wind was at the time you called — if nothing changes, what runway will you use, and which way will you turn off to get to the general aviation ramp?

Figure 6-3. Airport diagram, Olympia

Progressive Taxi

When at an airport you are unfamiliar with, you should ask the ground controller for "progressive taxi" instructions at your first contact after switching from the tower frequency on arrival, or on your first call when departing. After landing at such an airport you would say,

PILOT "Knoxville Ground, Piper 70497 at intersection Bravo Two, request progressive taxi to the general aviation ramp."

This is especially useful at night, when the airport environment seems to be a sea of blue lights. The controller will lead you by the hand:

GROUND "Turn right there…taxi across the runway and turn left at the first taxiway on the other side…"

The ground controller will tell you where the fixed base operations are but will not recommend one over another — that has to be your decision.

Departures

When departing, you won't say anything to the local controller until you have completed your runup and are in position at the hold line, ready to taxi onto the active runway:

PILOT "Boeing Tower, Baron 1014W ready for takeoff on 31 left, VFR westbound [downwind departure, staying in the pattern]."

If you hear,

TOWER "Baron 1014W cleared for takeoff."

— it isn't even necessary to reply; just get on the throttle and go. The controller will accept the fact that you are moving onto the runway as acknowledgment. If, however, you hear,

TOWER "Baron 14W cleared for immediate takeoff or hold short."

— stop and think for a moment. That clearance means that someone is on final approach, and the local controller wants you to either get moving right away or stay off the runway. The smart thing to do is to wait. Pilots who are in a hurry make mistakes. If, on the other hand, you are confident that you are really ready to go, don't pick up the mike, but push on the throttle. The delay while you reach for the mike and acknowledge the instructions might eliminate the gap in traffic that the controller was counting on. At a busy airport with ten planes in the pattern and five behind you in the runup area, be ready to go without acknowledgment but still acknowledge the clearance as soon as you can. (See the discussion of boom mikes in Chapter 2 on Page 8.)

Hold Short

Most of the time, action speaks louder than words. When the controller tells you to turn base, reaching for the microphone is a waste of time — just turn base and the controller will be able to see you complying. Grab the mike and acknowledge when the wings are level. The same is true of a takeoff clearance. Of all the things available for your use in the cockpit, the microphone is the least important when it comes to flying the airplane.

There is a special case that calls for a response, however. If the controller tells you to hold short of the runway your response must include the words "hold short." Clicking the mike or saying "Roger" won't do the job.

PILOT **"Piper 497 holding short of 29"**

— this has to go on the tower's tape recorder for legal reasons.

Equally important, if you are inbound to an airport that has intersecting runways and the tower controller says,

TOWER **"...cleared to land runway 16, hold short of runway 24"**

— you *must* consider your speed, altitude, aircraft configuration, and proficiency, and if you are not absolutely certain that you will be able to bring your airplane to a controlled stop before reaching the intersection you must say "Unable." That will give the controller an opportunity to change plans and give you alternative instructions. Smoking the brakes as you skid through the intersection is definitely bad form.

"Taxi into Position and Hold"

"Taxi into position and hold" means just that, but don't put your brain in neutral when you are sitting on the runway in takeoff position. Listen to the tower frequency — did the controller just clear someone to land on the same runway that you are parked on? If so, you should get takeoff clearance in a matter of seconds, not minutes. The *Air Traffic Control Manual* has been modified recently to require that all "Taxi into position" pilots be advised of any traffic that has been cleared to land on that runway.

Some pilots feel more comfortable taking a position 90 degrees to the runway so that they can see the final approach course. If you want to do this, be sure to advise the controller of your intentions — the sequence of landing traffic is based on your being aligned with the runway.

You will not get a "position and hold" instruction at night; you may recall that a 737 landed on a commuter that was holding in position for takeoff at night.

Wake Turbulence

Another possible transmission from the tower controller is,

> TOWER **"Piper 70497 taxi into position and hold, expect three minute delay for wake turbulence."**

You can waive the delay, if you are feeling especially brave.

> PILOT **"497 will waive the delay"**

…will get you a takeoff clearance. After telling the local controller what you intend to do, a 90-degree turn into the wind as soon as practicable will take you away from most potential wake turbulence. Don't maintain runway heading — the turbulence descends below the generating airplane and you can't possibly outclimb a jet.

Don't anticipate what the tower controller is going to say — if you do, you will hear what you expect to hear, not what is actually said. If you are #1 at the hold line, expecting to hear,

> TOWER **"Taxi into position and hold,"**

and the controller says,

> TOWER **"Taxi across without delay and hold short on the other side,"**

…you might taxi into takeoff position on the runway through force of habit. When in doubt, ask. The 747 taxiing up behind you can wait 30 seconds while you clear things up with the controller.

Intersection Takeoffs

The tower controller will let you take off from an intersection if that is what you want to do, and in many cases you will be cleared to taxi to an intersection for takeoff. You are entirely within your rights to say,

> PILOT **"Baron 1014W requests the full length."**

…and in my judgment that is usually the best policy, unless you have 5,000 or 6,000 feet of runway available from the intersection. It's always nice to have runway in front of you if the engine decides to make funny noises or the door pops open just after takeoff.

When you are ready for takeoff from an intersection, be sure to include your position when calling the tower:

> PILOT **"Flying Cloud tower, Cessna 1357X ready for takeoff on 9 Right at Golf."**

The tower controller has a lot of real estate to monitor and might not pick up your little airplane visually without a little help.

Trivia note: Ground controllers never use the word "cleared," and you should not ask for a taxi clearance. The ground controller uses phrases like "taxi to runway 13," "taxi across runway 27," and so forth but does not issue clearances. Only the local controller can issue clearances.

"Request Frequency Change"

When you depart an airport with an operating control tower you are obligated to stay on the tower frequency until you cross the boundary of Class D airspace as depicted on your sectional chart. It is not necessary to request a frequency change as you leave Class D airspace, although for some reason many pilots do. This just makes additional work for the controller, who is busy enough as it is. The great majority of instructors teach their students to do this, although I can't imagine why.

If there is a possibility of conflict, the controller may say "Cessna 1357X stay with me," as you approach the boundary of Delta airspace, following up with "change to advisory frequency approved" when the conflict has been resolved.

You want to think long and hard before requesting a frequency change while still within the Class D surface area as indicated on the Sectional Chart; the tower might need to warn you of conflicting traffic. The usual terminology is,

> CONTROLLER **"Change to advisory frequency approved"**

— leaving the decision up to you as to whether you want to ask ATC for flight following or shift to UNICOM. Of course, you don't have to talk to anyone while cruising along in Class E airspace.

Blocked Frequency

Very infrequently you will be faced with a situation where, because of a stuck mike on the frequency or other equipment failure, you are unable to make contact with the local or ground controller. Use your knowledge of the airport or the A/FD to get around this type of problem:

> PILOT "Boeing Tower, Cessna 1357X, unable to contact ground control, at south parking to taxi to 13L."

> PILOT "Santa Maria Ground, Cessna 1357X, unable to contact tower, over Lompoc to land Santa Maria."

> PILOT "Portland Clearance Delivery [from A/FD], Cessna 1357X, unable to contact ground, at Flightcraft to taxi 10L."

Special Visual Flight Rules (SVFR)

You will need a Special VFR clearance to enter or leave the surface area of Class D airspace as depicted on your sectional chart, just as you do when Class E airspace extends to the ground. The clearance will be much easier to obtain at a tower-controlled airport than at an airport in Class E airspace simply because the communications links between towers and radar facilities are better.

If you are departing an airport where the current ceiling is less than 1,000 feet or the current visibility is less than 3 miles and you are not instrument rated, your call to ground control should be:

> PILOT "Boeing Ground, Baron 1014W, [position on the airport], request Special VFR clearance."

You should *never* ask for such a clearance unless you are absolutely certain that the poor conditions are localized and that you will encounter good VFR flight conditions before you cross the boundary of Class D airspace as shown on the sectional chart. Your clearance will sound something like this:

> GROUND "Baron 1014W is cleared out of the Boeing Delta airspace to the northwest, maintain Special VFR conditions at or below 1,300 feet. Report clear of the Delta surface area."

When you look ahead and see that the area around your destination airport is covered by low clouds, the tower controller will probably reply to your initial call with:

> TOWER **"Piper 70497, Boeing Field is currently below VFR minimums, say your intentions?"**

Your reply should be:

> PILOT **"497 requests Special VFR clearance into your Delta airspace,"**

and not, "I want to land."

Controllers cannot solicit SVFR; no controller will ever say "Would you like a Special VFR clearance?"

Again, you will have to read the SVFR clearance back verbatim, so be ready to copy.

> TOWER **"Piper 70497 is cleared into the Boeing Field Delta airspace from the northwest, maintain Special VFR conditions at or below 1,300 feet, report entering Delta airspace."**

In case you are wondering what the "at or below 1,300 feet" is all about, the floor of Class B airspace for Seattle-Tacoma International Airport overlies Boeing Field at 1,300 feet and SeaTac is one of the airports at which no fixed-wing Special VFR is permitted in Class B airspace. You can expect similar restrictions at other airports based on local airspace allocations.

Satellite Airports in Class D Airspace

The sectional chart excerpt shows several small airports that are located within the boundaries of Class D airspace for larger airports: Martha Lake at Paine Field, Aero Plaza at Olympia, and Spanaway at McChord AFB are examples of satellite airports. A pilot who wants to takeoff or land at a satellite airport must establish communications with the tower at the primary airport. In the case of a departure, if the tower cannot be contacted from the ground the pilot must contact the tower as soon as possible after departure.

Whether or not you need a Special VFR clearance to operate into or from a satellite airport is a function of the weather at the primary airport, not the satellite.

For example, if the Paine Field weather is below basic VFR minimums, a pilot who desires to land at Martha Lake must obtain a SVFR clearance to do so from Paine Tower, even if Martha Lake's weather is clear and a million. Similarly, to takeoff from Martha Lake when Paine is reporting weather below basic VFR, a pilot must communicate with Paine Tower and get an SVFR clearance.

Figure 6-4. Olympia Airport, Washington

Arriving At Olympia

Your cross-country trip is almost over as you can see the south end of Puget Sound ahead and you know that the Olympia airport lies a few miles futher south.

You cannot enter Olympia's Class D airspace until you have established two-way communications with the tower controller; the boundaries of the Class D airspace are printed on your chart (Figure 6-4 and Airport C on the chart excerpt). You should be monitoring the tower frequency when you are no less than ten miles away from the boundary, up by Boston Harbor. When you give yourself a 10 to 15 mile buffer you can listen to tower communications with other aircraft and get an idea of what is going on. You can also hear other airplanes reporting in and get an idea of where you will fit into the inbound flow. If you are north of the airport on V-287 and hear the tower tell another airplane,

TOWER "**Runway 36 cleared for takeoff, right crosswind departure approved**"

— you know that airplane will be heading your way.

Your initial call must include your full callsign position in relation to the airport or a geographic reporting point. Not a point that you see over the nose, but what you see when looking straight down. Choose a reporting point that the controller will be able to recognize. "Over the water tower" is not much use if there are six water towers in the vicinity. "Over the blue water tower at the southeast end of Beacon Hill" would be better.

PILOT "**Olympia Tower, Piper 70497 ten miles north for landing [or touch-and-go]**"

…should get a reply something like,

TOWER "**Piper 497, Olympia Tower, zero degree entry approved, report abeam the tower on left downwind, Olympia ceiling 6,000 broken, visibility 10, wind 340° at 6 knots, altimeter 30.11, runway 36 cleared to land.**"

(Olympia does not have an ATIS.)

This gives you permission to fly directly into the downwind leg (zero-degree entry) without making a 45. The controller could just as easily have said,

TOWER "**70497, Olympia Tower, runway 36 cleared to land. Report on the 45…**"

Have you noticed that in each of the examples the words "cleared to land" come last? That's because the FAA became aware that as soon as some pilots heard the word "cleared," their brains shut down and they didn't hear anything that followed. That is, of course, why ground controllers never use that word.

Once you are safely on the ground at Olympia you can switch over to 122.2 Mhz, the standard FSS frequency, and say,

PILOT "**Seattle Radio, Piper 70497 on the ground at Olympia. Please close my flight plan at 45 past the hour.**"

Once again, you have been bailed out by that Airport/Facility Directory I've been hounding you about. In the explanation of the airport listing legend, under "Communications," it says that 122.2 is assigned to most FSS's as a common enroute simplex service. The frequency 123.6 is used at non-tower airports.

Strange Airport Arrival

If you are arriving at a controlled airport you are unfamiliar with, tell the controller in the first transmission:

> PILOT "Addison Tower, Baron 1014W approximately 8 miles south with information Romeo, unfamiliar."

This will get the message across. A sharp controller will then say something like,

> TOWER "Baron 14W, do you see a brown office building at your one o'clock, five miles? Report abeam that building"

…and when the building is off your right wing tip you will say,

> PILOT "Addison Tower, 14W abeam the building."

The controllers have a variety of such reporting points selected, so that they can serve traffic inbound from just about any direction, and when you make that report you should be in position to at least see the runway, if not land straight in.

Including your altitude in the initial call won't do much for the tower controller, but it might be useful information for other airplanes in your vicinity. Nothing makes you scrunch up in your seat like hearing someone else report that they are at your position and altitude. On the other hand, if the other pilot reports over the north end of Dog Island at 1,500 feet when you are also over the north end of Dog Island but at 1,000 feet you can notify both the tower and the other pilot of the potential conflict by transmitting:

> PILOT "Tower, 14W is also over the north end of Dog Island, level at 1,000 feet."

The tower will then verify that the higher airplane has the lower airplane in sight and will caution both pilots to maintain visual separation and/or direct one pilot to follow the other one.

In the Pattern and on Final Approach

Many busy airports have two or more tower frequencies assigned. The ATIS will say something like,

> ATIS "Arrivals from the northeast contact Bigtown Tower on 118.3, arrivals from the west contact Bigtown Tower on 120.2."

A tower equipped with a BRITE radar display can see the transponder returns from VFR traffic, although the controllers cannot give vectors;

> CONTROLLER "Piper 497, suggested heading to the downwind leg is 230."

This is not a vector. The BRITE display is a tremendous tool when the sky seems full of airplanes all headed for the downwind leg.

Tower controllers who must space traffic using binoculars or the Mark I eyeball have the problem of parallax, or difficulty in visually separating two targets along a line of sight:

> TOWER **"Piper 497, turn left immediately, fly a wide downwind and follow the Baron off your right wing"**

— is a transmission that might be heard when the pilot of the Piper has the Baron in sight a half-mile ahead, while to the controller they appear about to collide. In this situation, the pilot of the airplane farthest from the pattern has a better picture of the situation than the tower controller.

> PILOT **"Tower, 497 has the traffic in sight ahead and will follow that traffic."**

This is a clue to the controller that the spacing is not as tight as it appears. On the other hand, if tower instructions to enter the pattern on a 45 will put you in conflict with an airplane already on downwind you must take immediate action and then tell the tower what you are doing:

> PILOT **"Tower, 497 is turning downwind outside of the traffic and will slow to follow it"**

…is one suggestion. If you wonder why your instructor has you practice transitioning from pattern entry speed to slow flight and back again, this is the explanation. Don't do any maneuvering without a clearance from the tower; the controller might have plans for the airplane following you that do not take into account the possibility that you will do an unannounced 360-degree turn for spacing. If you reduce your airspeed, the following pilot should see that the distance in trail is diminishing and follow suit.

When your position is such that you can enter the pattern on the base leg or even straight-in to the downwind (a "zero-degree" entry), don't hesitate to ask up front:

> PILOT **"Tower, Cessna 1357X six miles north, request left base entry"**

— or,

> PILOT **"Tower, Cessna 1357X six miles north, request straight-in to the downwind."**

In either case, the tower controller can simply turn you down:

> TOWER **"Cessna 1357X, enter on the 45; report when on the 45"**

but chances are that your request will be granted:

TOWER "**57X, cleared as requested, report two mile left base**"

— or,

TOWER "**57X, cleared as requested, report two miles north for downwind entry.**"

By the way, that "two mile left base" report means two miles from the extended centerline of the landing runway; some pilots interpret it to mean that the base leg should be adjusted so that it intersects the final approach course two miles from the runway. Look at it from the controller's point of view: if you report on base when two miles from the extended centerline, the controller knows where to look.

A zero-degree entry to the downwind exposes you to traffic turning crosswind after departure as well as traffic entering on the 45 too close to the departure end of the pattern. It's a timesaver, but you have to keep your head on a swivel.

Always be at the published pattern altitude (in the A/FD) well before entry to avoid any high wing/low wing conflicts. Sometimes you can pick up the silhouette of other traffic against the sky, but more often than not you will be trying to pick a moving target out of a fixed background of ground structures.

Student pilots should always identify themselves as students when contacting air traffic controllers. It can't hurt, and it might help. A rapid-fire string of instructions answered with "say again, please" just won't happen if the controller realizes that slow and easy will work better.

Never be reluctant to tell a controller that you are unfamiliar with the area. Many, many pilots have blundered into the airspace of the wrong airport before confessing their confusion to ATC (and some have even landed at the wrong airport). You will receive instructions that refer to readily identifiable landmarks instead of "report crossing Washington Street."

Estimating distances is difficult at best. You do know how long the landing runway is, however. For example, reporting a two mile final to a 5,000-foot-long runway would require you to mentally extend the runway two runway-lengths toward your position.

If the wind is gusty and variable, don't be reluctant to ask the tower controller for a wind check on short final; remember, the ATIS might not reflect current conditions. A simple—

PILOT "**Tower, 57X, wind check**"

— will do.

Adjusting The Pattern

During your flight training, the point at which you turned from downwind to base was your own decision. At a tower controlled airport there are a couple of situations in which that turn point might be dictated by the controller. How about:

> TOWER "Baron 1014W, follow the Cessna on final, cleared to land."

If you don't see the airplane on final you might say,

> PILOT "Not in sight, call my base."

But it's not always a pilot request. When a busy pattern has been stretched out to an unacceptable length, the controller might try to get things back to normal by saying to a pilot on downwind,

> TOWER "Baron 14W in sight, continue on downwind, number three to land, I'll call your base."

In each case, simply identify yourself and say "Wilco."

At a controlled airport, is it necessary to make the base and final reports that you make at uncontrolled airports? In theory, the fact that the controller has responsibility for the airspace should relieve you of that duty. However, if you hear something on the frequency that smacks of a potential conflict, speak up — tower controllers aren't perfect. If you hear another airplane cleared to occupy the airspace that you are currently occupying, tell the tower.

At airports with parallel runways, the pilot of an airplane on a straight-in final to one runway (completing an instrument approach, for example), might be concerned to see you in position to cross its path.

> PILOT "Baron 14W turning final for 13L has the traffic on final for the right"

…will lower that pilot's anxiety level.

You're the boss when it comes to the operation of your airplane. That's difficult for low-time pilots to accept, but it is right there in the Federal Aviation Regulations. You must add "negative" and "unable" to your vocabulary. Abusing the brakes to comply with an instruction to turn at the next intersection is potentially much more expensive than saying "unable," because on a slick runway you might lose control of the airplane. Keep in mind that the controller does not have to pay for any damage you do to your airplane and will go home with a clear conscience.

This is equally true when you get clearances like "Make short approach," "Cleared to land runway 36, hold short of runway 27," and things like that. Don't make extravagant efforts to comply with controller instructions that will stretch your abilities, and the capabilities of your airplane, to their limits.

If you are given a "land and hold short (of a crossing runway)" instruction and there is any doubt whatsoever about your ability to get your airplane on the ground and stopped before reaching the crossing runway, let the controller know as soon as possible so that airplanes using the crossing runway can be spaced accordingly. This is not a situation in which you want to surprise the controller.

When appropriate, suggest alternative actions. If runway 36 is the active, but runway 30 will get you to the ramp with less taxi time, ask the controller for clearance to land on 30 instead.

PILOT **"Tower, Cessna 1357X requests 30"**

— will do the trick if the controller thinks that no compromise to safety will result. The same holds true for departures. Traffic and wind permitting, you can take off on any runway you choose—a tower controller cannot deny you a takeoff clearance. Of course, you might have to sit and stew for a long time while everyone else takes off on the preferred runway, but your time will come if you are patient.

Every year, FAA air traffic controllers at Wittman Field in Oshkosh, Wisconsin, turn its 8,000-foot-long runway into two end-to-end 4,000-foot runways. One pilot will be cleared to land on the numbers, while the next will be told to maintain altitude while flying down the first half and to land past the midpoint. No one taxis to an intersection, they just turn off into the grass and are directed to parking. For one week, Oshkosh becomes the busiest airport in the world, with over 15,000 airplanes coming in to land.

When you hear a tower controller say something like,

TOWER **"57X, make midfield base south of the tower, cleared to land on the last half,"**

(or, when you are on final) —

TOWER **"Keep your altitude up, land on the last half of the runway"**

…it's not something unusual, but it is a tested procedure that can expedite your landing.

Check to see if your local pilot supply store has any audio tapes of tower communications at Oshkosh — listening to that activity will really open your eyes to how flexible aviation communication can be.

"Land long" is another phrase that can be used by either the pilot or the controller. Your airplane would rather fly than taxi, so why not fly down the runway to shorten taxi time when that is convenient?

PILOT "Tower, 57X requests long landing"

…is all it takes. A clearance to land long is not a sure thing — hearing,

TOWER "57X, unable, traffic waiting for midfield departure"

— is one possibility. If your home airport has a tower and the controller recognizes your N-number, you may hear,

TOWER "Cessna 57X, where do you park?"

followed by (if it would save you some taxi time),

TOWER "Cleared to land, long landing approved"

— (although you didn't ask for one).

When landing at an airport with parallel runways, don't be reluctant to turn from base to final just a little early to insure that your flight path will not encroach on the other runway's final approach path. This is a situation where those crisp 90-degree turns are not appropriate.

A tower controller may ask you to slow down, speed up, do S-turns for spacing, or even do a 360-degree turn for spacing on downwind or final. That's fine — do as requested if you can do so safely (or say "unable"). Do not do any maneuvers on your own authority just because it seems like the right thing to do; the controller has a landing sequence in mind and your well-intended maneuver might just throw a wrench into the works.

At a busy airport you may hear,

TOWER "57X, cancel landing clearance, go around at pattern altitude."

Unexpected, but not a big deal — just make your rectangular pattern at pattern altitude with the upwind leg right over the runway while the tower gets a couple of departures out.

PILOT "57X, Wilco."

If you are on final and getting too close to the airplane ahead, the tower controller may ask you to go around without overflying the other plane:

TOWER "57X, go around, overfly the west taxiway [or the grass]."

Again, you simply acknowledge with your callsign. "Wilco" is the official AIM response, but when the tower controller can see that you are complying it is superfluous.

Night Operations

A night landing at any airport can be a challenge, but if you know the magic words, a tower controller just might be able to make it easier. The instrument approach lights are normally turned on only when the ground visibility drops below two miles, but the controller will be happy to turn them on if you say something like,

PILOT **"Bigtown tower, request the approach lights and rabbit."**

The "rabbit" is a system of sequenced flashing lights that can't be mistaken for anything else and it leads directly to the threshold (this works in the daytime, too). Runway End Identifier Lights are two lights placed on either side of an instrument runway that flash regularly; if the runway is not served by a rabbit, the REIL will do the trick. The controller can also vary the intensity of the runway lights on request.

As you know, not all tower controlled airports are 24-hour facilities. You should be able to control the approach and runway lights by keying your microphone the correct number of times on the correct frequency. Find the details on a specific airport in the Airport/Facilities Directory, a reference you should not be without.

Landing Alternatives

Most of your landings at controlled airports will be full stops or touch-and-goes. Make sure that the controller knows what your needs are well in advance. If you intend to land and taxi back, or just quit for the day, and the controller says,

TOWER **"Cleared for touch and go"**

…be sure to respond with,

PILOT **"1357X is full stop."**

Although the alternatives I am about to suggest are more for instructors than for students or certified pilots, you should be familiar with them.

The first is "stop and go." When practicing landings, you might want to bring the airplane to a full stop, configure for takeoff, and then commence your takeoff. You clue the controller by asking for a stop-and-go, so that spacing between your airplane and following airplanes can be adjusted.

The next is "cleared for the option," and you get it by saying:

PILOT **"Tower, 1357X requests the option."**

When you are cleared for the option you can make a touch-and-go, a stop-and-go, or a full stop; the controller will give you time and space for any of the above.

NORDO

Operating at a tower-controlled airport without a radio is legal, but it places an undue load on the controllers and should be avoided if possible. Handheld radios aren't that expensive. This book is intended for pilots with radios installed in their airplanes.

What if your radio breaks down in flight? The smart thing to do is to land at an uncontrolled airport and call your destination tower on the telephone, giving your airplane type, color, and your estimated time of arrival. Then just fly into the pattern, blinking your landing light and waggling your wings until you get a green light from the tower. You could do the flashing-lights and wing-waggle bit without the phone call, but it isn't good form to do so. (*See* Chapter 12 for more about emergency procedures.)

Departing a Satellite Airport

When you are departing from a small airport that lies within the boundaries of Class D airspace, you are required to contact the control tower at the primary airport from the ground before takeoff if that is possible:

> PILOT **"Bigtown Tower, Piper 70497 ready for takeoff at Littlefield, VFR westbound."**

If you cannot contact the tower from the ground, you must do so as soon as possible after departure:

> PILOT **"Bigtown Tower, Piper 70497 off from Littlefield, through 500 for 2,500, VFR westbound."**

In either case, the tower will acknowledge your call and give you traffic information.

If your destination airport lies within the boundaries of Class D airspace, you must establish communication with the tower just as if you were going to land at the primary airport. The only exception is that you say:

> PILOT **"Bigtown Tower, Piper 70497 six miles southeast with information Mike, landing Littlefield."**

The tower will simply acknowledge your call and give you any pertinent traffic information. Do not expect to receive a clearance to land — the tower controller does not have any clearance authority at the satellite airport.

Just Passing Through

If you want to fly through Class D airspace there is no reason why you shouldn't. Remember that Delta airspace only extends 2,500 feet above airport elevation, though, and that no communication is *required* if you fly overhead at an altitude higher than that ceiling. However, if you are any lower and on radar flight following, it wouldn't hurt to check with the controller to be sure that any necessary coordination has been accomplished.

> PILOT "Approach [or Center], 1357X, am I cleared through Bigtown's Delta airspace?"

(The AIM and the *Air Traffic Control Manual* differ slightly on this, so call to be on the safe side.) Monitoring the tower frequency would be a great idea, however. You might hear something like:

> TOWER "Baron 14W is cleared for takeoff; there is a Cessna one mile south of the airport, eastbound, indicating 3,000 feet, but we're not talking to him."

Or, you might hear,

> TOWER "Cessna 1357X there is a Learjet at your two o'clock on final for runway 6."

That would be your clue to keep an eye on the Learjet until it was well clear of your flightpath, or you could volunteer:

> PILOT "Tower, Cessna 1357X has the Learjet visually and will pass well clear."

The best place to cross an airport is overhead and at right angles to the threshold of the active runway. Planes landing or taking off will be either on the runway or very close to it at that point. If your desired penetration altitude will be within 2,500 feet of the surface, just call the tower well outside of the Class D airspace and say,

> PILOT "Bigtown Tower, Cessna 1357X request clearance through your airspace at [your desired MSL altitude],"

…and the tower will reply with something like,

> TOWER "57X cleared as requested, cross the upwind end of [active runway] at [assigned altitude] and report when clear."

Some busy airports have VFR flyways designed to enable VFR flights to get around or through the tower's airspace with a minimum of disruption; these flyways are printed on the reverse of the Terminal Area Charts for the airports involved. Pilots must still communicate with the tower (or Approach Control — the Terminal Area Chart will have the details), but at least they know that there is a route reserved for VFR operations and that their chances of getting across the airport are much better using the flyway than by using a "roll-your-own" route.

Los Angeles International is a special case. It not only has *two* flyways, but it also has a "Special Flight Rules Area." Pilots using the SFRA are not required to communicate with ATC and do not require a clearance of any kind through the Class B airspace — but they must have a current Terminal Area Chart in the cockpit because that is where all of the operational details will be found. A discrete frequency is assigned solely for the use of pilots transiting the SFRA, so that they can talk to one another and avoid any conflicts in this very small corridor.

When Your Eyes Deceive You

Occasionally, the FAA will establish a temporary control tower at an airport in Class G or E airspace for an airshow or a fly-in. The existence of these towers is promulgated through Notices and Letters to Airmen, but there is obviously no change to the relevant sectional chart. Still, when a temporary tower is in operation it brings Class D airspace with it. If you fail to communicate with the tower before landing at such an airport and get a violation, "It wasn't on the chart" will not be accepted as a defense.

UNICOM at Tower-Controlled Airports

Almost all of the tower-controlled airports on the sectional chart excerpt show a frequency of 122.95, which is a UNICOM frequency. Does this mean that you can bypass the tower controller and ask UNICOM for the runway in use? No way. UNICOM is provided at tower-controlled airports for many of the same reasons it is provided at small airports: calling for fuel, calling a cab, or notifying someone of your ETA, but not for traffic or weather information. Most UNICOM operators at tower-controlled airports can't see the runway or the traffic pattern from their offices and have no weather reporting instruments, so you won't be using UNICOM for anything other than the types of transmissions listed above.

Summary

When the tower is in operation, two-way radio communication is required in Class D airspace (or in Class E or even Class G if a temporary tower has been established by Notice to Airmen). When the tower is closed, the airspace becomes either Class E (full-time weather observer) or Class G. In less than VFR conditions, operation in Class D or E airspace requires an SVFR clearance. Inbound, call the local controller well in advance of crossing the blue dashed line.

7 Class C Airspace

Radar Required

The FAA designates airports as Class C airspace when radar control is available and the airspace is congested (but not sufficiently congested to warrant Class B status). The old name was Airport Radar Service Area, and that name pretty well told the tale. (*See* Figure 7-1 on the next page.)

Before you can take off from or land at the primary airport or fly through the Class C airspace, you must establish two-way communications with the controlling facility.

When Class C is Not Class C

Since the FAA completed the changeover to the new system of airspace designations in September, 1993, it has been difficult for pilots to determine if a given Class C location was in effect full time or part-time. In the case of part-time Class C airspace, it has been equally difficult to tell what kind of airspace remains when Class C is not in effect. During 1995, the information panels on Sectional and Terminal Area Charts will be revised to show "Class B, Class C, and Selected Radar Approach Control Frequencies," and the column headed "Service Availability" will add the type of airspace that the Class C airspace reverts to. (See the table example in Figure 7-2, and Airport K on the sectional chart excerpt at the back of the book.)

You will notice on the chart excerpt that there is no blue dashed line around Spokane International Airport (Airport H on the chart excerpt) and the adjacent Fairchild AFB, although both have towers. The Class C airspace is effective full-time at those airports, and because the terminal radar facility works hand-in-glove with the control tower, there is no Class D airspace as such. Look just south-southeast of the Whidbey Island Class C airspace (Airport K) for the notation "See NOTAMs/ Directory for Class E (sfc) eff hrs"; the revised table will clarify this notation.

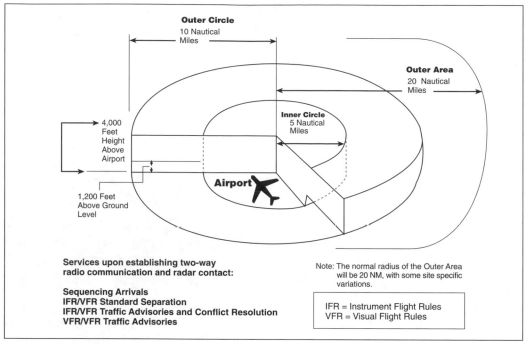

Services upon establishing two-way
radio communication and radar contact:

Sequencing Arrivals
IFR/VFR Standard Separation
IFR/VFR Traffic Advisories and Conflict Resolution
VFR/VFR Traffic Advisories

Note: The normal radius of the Outer Area
will be 20 NM, with some site specific
variations.

IFR = Instrument Flight Rules
VFR = Visual Flight Rules

Figure 7-1. Class C airspace

Class B, Class C, TRSA and Selected Radar Approach Control Frequencies	Service Availability
Seattle Class B RWY 16/34 119.2 284.7 (341° - 075°) RWY 16/34 120.1 290.9 (199° - 300°) RWY 16 119.2 284.7 (076° - 160°) RWY 16 125.9 290.9 (301° - 340°) RWY 34 125.9 290.9 (076° - 160°) RWY 34 120.4 395.0 (301° - 340°) RWY 16/34 126.5 391.9 (161° - 198°)	
Fairchild AFB/ Spokane Class C 123.75 384.9 (205° - 025°) 133.35 263.0 (026° - 204°)	
Portland Class C 118.1 284.6 (100° - 279°) 133.0 360.8 (280° - 099°)	
Whidbey Island Class C 118.2 286.0 (West) 120.7 270.8 (East)	Whidbey Island Class E 0800 - 1500Z

Special Use Airspace on Seattle Sectional Chart

Unless otherwise noted altitudes are
MSL and in feet; time is local.
Contact nearest FSS for information.
†Other time by NOTAM contact FSS

The word "To" an altitude means "To and including."
"Mon-Fri" indicates "Monday through Friday"
FL = Flight Level
NO A/G = No air to ground communications

Figure 7-2. Service availability

Transponder Use

Because Class C airspace is designated where a terminal radar is available, pilots must have an operable transponder with Modes A and C in their aircraft for identification.

More often than not, ATC controllers will assign a discrete transponder code for use while in their airspace. Many instructors tell their students that it is not necessary to acknowledge ATC instructions to change transponder codes or IDENT because the controller will see the change on the radar scope. However, controllers are quick to point out that they have other things to do in addition to watching for your data block, and that several seconds may elapse before the change shows up on the scope. Moral: Always back up transponder changes with a voice transmission —

> CONTROLLER **"Piper 70497, squawk 6723 and ident."**

> PILOT **"497 squawking 6723"**

— will do the trick.

Arrival

The "outer area" of Class C airspace extends 20 nautical miles from the primary airport and affords you the opportunity to make contact with the controlling ATC facility well in advance of entry into the inner area, 10 miles in radius, where participation is mandatory. Take advantage of it — call approach control 15 to 20 miles out so that you can devote all of your attention to flying the airplane and checking for traffic. Bear in mind that you cannot enter the inner 10-mile circle without having established communication with ATC. The Class C airspace at Spokane International Airport (Figure 7-3 and Airport H on the chart excerpt) is a good example; you get the frequencies from a panel on the Sectional chart or from the A/FD:

> PILOT **"Spokane Approach, Baron 1014W 20 miles west, 7,500 feet with November, landing Spokane International."**

> APPROACH **"Baron 14W, Spokane Approach, maintain present heading, descend and maintain 6,000 feet, squawk 4657."**

> PILOT **"Leaving 7.5 for 6, 4657, 14W."**

Although you do not need a clearance in order to enter Class C airspace, when Approach Control has established radar contact and you are talking to each other, you must comply with any heading or altitude changes directed by Approach. This is a real advantage to a pilot who is a stranger to the area, because the controller can

Continued on Page 7-6

Figure 7-3. Spokane International Airport, Washington

APPROACH "Baron 1014W, radar service terminated, squawk 1200 and contact Felts Tower on 132.5."

Figure 7-4. Felts Field, Spokane, Washington

provide vectors to the pattern or to the final approach course. After coordinating with the control tower, the approach controller will give you the tower frequency and tell you to contact the tower. What could be easier?

Essentially the same conversation would take place if Baron 14W intended to land at Felts Field, outside of the 5 mile inner circle (Figure 7-4 and Airport I on the chart excerpt). Spokane Approach would hand off 14W to the Felts tower as soon as it was clear of the inner circle and advise the pilot to contact the tower:

APPROACH "**Baron 1014W, radar service terminated, squawk 1200 and contact Felts Tower on 132.5.**"

Departure

When you depart the primary airport in Class C airspace you are required to establish two-way communication with ATC, and your normal contacts with ground control and the tower meet this requirement. You may receive specific instructions from the tower —

TOWER "**After takeoff turn right heading 030, climb and maintain 2,500 feet**"

— to keep your flight separated from other departures.

When you are departing Class C airspace, give ATC a call upon leaving the outer circle (10 miles out):

PILOT "**14W requests terminate radar service**"

…which will bring,

CONTROLLER "**Baron 14W, position 11 miles southeast of Bigtown, radar service terminated, squawk one two zero zero. Frequency change approved.**"

If you do not make this call, the radar facility must continue to provide traffic vectors or traffic advisories until your radar target leaves the outer area (20 miles out). ATC's final transmission will be the same.

In addition to staying on the right side of the law, being in contact with ATC in Class C airspace can really help when you approach a strange airport; just ask for vectors to the pattern.

PILOT "**Bigtown Approach, Baron 14W is unfamiliar, request vectors to the pattern.**"

More often than not, this will result in your being placed in position for a straight-in approach, but will on occasion place you on downwind. The last transmission you will hear from the radar controller will be,

APPROACH **"Baron 14W, contact tower 118.1."**

The tower controller will have been alerted by interphone and will know where to look for you when you make your call:

PILOT **"Bigtown Tower, Baron 14W on the 45 for 13 left."**

SVFR

If the ceiling is below 1,000 feet and/or the visibility is less than 3 miles, you must either go IFR, or ask ATC for a Special VFR clearance, just as in Class D airspace. To accept such a clearance the visibility must be at least one mile and you must be able to stay clear of clouds while within the surface area of the Class C airspace. I've hedged on identifying the type of visibility because it depends on whether or not there is an observer at the airport to report ground visibility. If there is, the ground visibility must be at least one mile, and if there isn't, then flight visibility governs.

Satellite Airports

When departing a satellite airport in Class C airspace you must contact ATC as soon as practicable after takeoff:

PILOT **"Bigtown Approach, Piper 70497 just off from Littleburg, 1,500 climbing 3,500."**

You will be asked to either IDENT on code 1200 or change to a discrete code, then:

APPROACH **"497, radar contact, report level 3,500."**

If you intend to land at a satellite airport inside Class C airspace, simply advise ATC on initial contact:

PILOT **"Bigtown Approach, Piper 70497 15 miles northwest, landing Littleburg."**

Remember that a column of airspace extending from airport elevation to 10,000 feet MSL and 20 miles in diameter extends above the primary airport in every Class C airspace. The only direct impact this has on your operation is that you must have a Mode C encoding transponder when transiting this column of airspace. The bottom 4,000 feet of this column of air (or as charted) is the Class C airspace where two-way communication with ATC is required.

"Piper 70497, Stand By"

There is a loophole in Class C procedures that I am honor-bound to tell you about, although I personally would not take advantage of it. If you are inbound to a Class C airport and say,

PILOT "Podunk Approach, Piper 70497, ten miles northeast, landing."

...and the controller says,

APPROACH "Aircraft calling Podunk Approach, stand by"

— you have no choice but to stay outside of the inner area until the controller has a chance to say,

APPROACH "Aircraft calling Podunk Approach, say again your callsign."

You will provide your callsign, of course, and everything will then proceed normally. If, however, the controller answers your initial call with,

APPROACH "Piper 70497, stand by"

...the AIM says that communications have been established (through the use of your callsign) and you can proceed into the Class C airspace. I wouldn't touch that one with a ten-foot pole. If the controller is too busy to handle your flight normally, having you barge into the Class C airspace is ludicrous. Even though the Federal Aviation Regulations let pilots do all sorts of things, many of those things may be marginally safe—but stupid. This is an example.

TRSAs

Terminal Radar Service Areas are on a par with dinosaur footprints — they are reminiscent of days gone by. Usually associated with military or joint-use airports, the existence of a TRSA tells you that radar services are available but not mandatory, and that the airport is not busy enough to warrant its designation as Class C airspace. TRSAs show up on sectional charts as black circles.

If your destination is an airport within a TRSA I strongly recommend that you take advantage of the services being offered. Forget whatever you have read about Class II or Class III service — those distinctions no longer exist. You will find the radar approach control frequency on your sectional chart. Dial it up and say,

PILOT "Yeager radar, Baron 1014W is 12 miles east, landing Yeager."

The radar controller will assign a discrete squawk, and acknowledge radar contact. You will be provided with traffic information and vectors to the pattern and then handed off to the tower controller. When directed to change to the tower, remember that the tower and radar controllers have been discussing you on the telephone and the tower controller knows all about you.

PILOT "Yeager Tower, Baron 1014W on left base [downwind, final] for runway 27"

TOWER "14W cleared to land [or follow the Belchfire on final]."

Departing an airport in a TRSA, you should once again use the radar services that are available to you. Use normal Class D airspace departure procedures, and when airborne, ask the tower for a frequency change to the radar control frequency; then ask the radar controller for VFR traffic advisories while leaving the TRSA. Respond to traffic advisories with "In sight" or "Negative contact, keep me advised." Do not use "no joy" or "tally ho" unless you flew for the RAF in World War II.

The radar controller will turn you loose by saying "Radar service terminated, squawk 1200, frequency change approved." Don't leave the TRSA frequency without asking the controller for the local Center frequency, because you just might be able to switch over to Center for radar flight following (*see* Chapter 5, Class E airspace).

PILOT "Metro Center, Baron 1014W is 8 miles northeast of Yeager, VFR at 4,500 feet. Request flight following to Bigburg."

CENTER "14W, Metro Center, radar contact, maintain VFR, advise any altitude changes."

If you want to simply fly through TRSA airspace you are free to do so without contacting anyone. However, if the ceiling permits flight under VFR but still holds you down to a relatively low altitude where you might come into conflict with traffic entering or departing the TRSA, a call to clarify your status would eliminate any doubt for the controller:

PILOT "Yeager radar, Baron 1014W is 8 miles west, will be flying through your airspace at 4,500 feet west to east."

CONTROLLER "14W, Yeager radar, squawk 0400, report clear."

Now the controller knows who you are, what you are up to, and does not have to worry about an unknown target suddenly mixing it up with the TRSA traffic. You will be sent back to code 1200 when you report clear of the TRSA.

Summary

Entry into Class C airspace requires that two-way radio communications be established between the pilot and the controlling radar facility. A transponder with altitude reporting capability is required. The outer area gives an inbound pilot plenty of time to get his or her act together before entering the inner area. Pilots operating to or from satellite airports must contact the controlling facility as soon as possible.

⑧ Class B Airspace

Clearance Required

This is the first discussion of an airspace classification that requires a specific clearance before any operation within its boundaries. Class B airspace exists at the very busiest airports in the country, and the FAA exercises strict control over operations in that airspace. It even has its own chart series, the Terminal Area Charts (TAC). Student pilots are not allowed to fly in Class B airspace without specific instruction and an instructor's endorsement in their logbooks. We'll assume for the purposes of this discussion that you hold at least a Private Pilot certificate as you fly toward a destination that is the primary airport for Class B airspace (a properly checked-out student will follow the same procedures, of course).

Many pilots who are uncertain of their ability to fly in congested airspace will fly many miles out of their way to avoid flight in Class B airspace. In my opinion, that is a mistake. You have the right to exercise the privileges of your certificate and should assert that right. Of course, if the ATC controllers workload is such that handling VFR flights would interfere with ATC's basic responsibility to handle IFR flights, they have the right to say "unable due to workload." Then you must fly the long way around, and you should include this possibility in your preflight planning.

If you are forced to circumnavigate Class B airspace, try to stay at least one mile away from its boundaries and at least 1,000 feet beneath its floor. The FAA determines the boundaries horizontally but distance measuring equipment (DME) measures slant range. When your DME reads 10.0 miles, you may be only 9.6 horizontal miles away from the primary airport (depending on altitude, of course), and violating the airspace boundary.

Don't try to fly over Class B airspace unless you can clear it by 2,000 feet or more — turbojets like to pop out of the top if they can climb rapidly enough.

You should have the appropriate Terminal Area Chart for a couple of reasons. First, the ATC frequencies are listed in more detail, and second, the charts show VFR reporting points that controllers want you to use.

Approach and Departure Control

The controllers you will be talking to in Class B airspace occupy hushed, almost totally darkened rooms near the control tower for the primary airport. The walls are lined with radar scopes, with a team of controllers at each position. The airspace is divided into sectors, and in most cases is divided vertically as well, so that the same geographic area may be covered by a high sector controller and a low sector controller. Each controller has several frequencies available (some are Ultra-High Frequencies for the military). *See* Figure 8-1.

You will find the Automated Terminal Information Service frequency for the primary airport on the chart (some airports have more than one ATIS). Try to copy the ATIS from as far away as possible so that you know which runways are in use; that may affect the frequency on which you make your initial contact. Select the ATIS frequency and break the squelch to see if you can pick the information out of the static. If you can't, try again in a few minutes. Waiting until the ATIS signal is strong enough to break the squelch deprives you of planning time. The ATIS broadcast might include the initial contact frequency, but you will be ahead of the game if you have checked the Airport/Facility Directory and the TAC.

Just Passing Through

Let's fly through the Class B airspace first. You've looked up the ATIS frequency and listened to the taped broadcast, now ask yourself what information a controller might need from a pilot who wants to fly through Class B airspace: Who, Where (including altitude), and What (intentions).

> PILOT "Metro Approach, Baron 1014W over the BIGTOWN VOR at 7,500 feet, request clearance eastbound through your Bravo airspace."

That transmission assumed that you listened on the approach control frequency and found it fairly quiet. If it was hard to get a word in edgewise you could try,

> PILOT "Metro Approach, Baron 1014W, request."

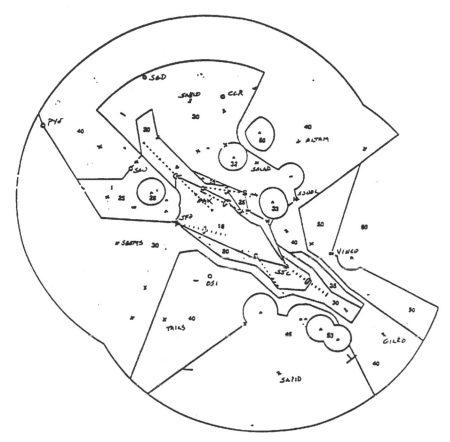

Figure 8-1. Bay approach sector chart (San Francisco, California)

That alerts the controller that you are on the frequency and want something. Your tail number will be added to the list of folks who want something, and the controller will get back to you as soon as practicable.

Your initial transmission didn't include a transponder squawk for a very good reason. If you were squawking anything other than 1200 it would be a discrete code assigned by ATC (an en route Center, most likely), and the whole handoff procedure would be handled between Center and Approach on the telephone. Center would tell you to contact Approach (and give you the correct frequency) and all you would have to do is switch frequencies and say,

PILOT "**Metro Approach, Baron 1014W, level at 7,500 VFR.**"

Your position, altitude, and intentions would have been passed along by the Center, but every controller wants to hear the altitude directly from you. Reminding the controller that you are VFR keeps that busy individual from riffling through a pile of flight strips looking for your IFR clearance. From this point on, passing through is just like landing at the primary airport; you just won't be turned over to the tower for landing instructions.

Landing at the Primary Airport

If you plan to land at the primary airport, make that clear in your initial transmission:

PILOT "Bigtown Approach, Piper 70497 10 miles northwest [or "over the freeway interchange"] with Kilo, landing Bigtown."

Try to use one of the charted VFR reporting points. Do not get closer than one mile to the boundary of the Class B airspace (two miles is much better) until you hear the words,

APPROACH "Piper 70497, radar contact, cleared to operate in the Bigtown Bravo airspace, maintain VFR."

"Radar contact" alone is not sufficient. Your response should be:

PILOT "Understand cleared into the Bravo airspace, 497."

If you are uncertain, ask:

PILOT "Is Piper 497 cleared into the Bravo airspace?"

Get your voice on the ATC tape recorder and make no assumptions — it is your pilot certificate on the line, not the controller's.

The boundaries of the Class B airspace that the controller sees on the scope are not as precise as what you can see by looking at objects on the surface, but if the controller decides that you have entered the airspace without a clearance, the government's computer record of radar images will prevail.

The Approach controller may ask you to squawk IDENT if you are on code 1200, assign a discrete code while in their airspace, or simply leave you on the code assigned by Center.

If you intend to land at the primary airport or at a satellite airport located within the Class B surface area, say,

PILOT "Metro Approach, Baron 1014W over the BIGTOWN VOR at 7,500 feet, landing at Metroplex International [or at Suburbia Municipal]."

Expect the controller to hand you off to the Metroplex International tower controller with no further action on your part:

APPROACH "Baron 1014W, contact Metro Tower 120.6"

PILOT "Roger, 120.6, 14W"

— or to vector you to the Suburbia pattern and turn you loose as soon as you report the field in sight:

APPROACH "Baron 1014W, squawk 1200, change to advisory frequency approved; good day."

Ideally, you should pick a VFR reporting point designated by a little magenta pennant on the Terminal Area Chart, or an actual photograph of a ground feature:

PILOT "Metro Approach, Baron 1014W over the stadium at 7,500 feet…"

…or give a direction and distance from the primary airport:

PILOT "Metro Approach, Baron 1014W, 18 miles northwest at 7,500 feet…"

If you are asked to IDENT, do so and confirm it by voice; the ATC radar antenna turns slowly enough that several seconds might go by before the controller notices your IDENT.

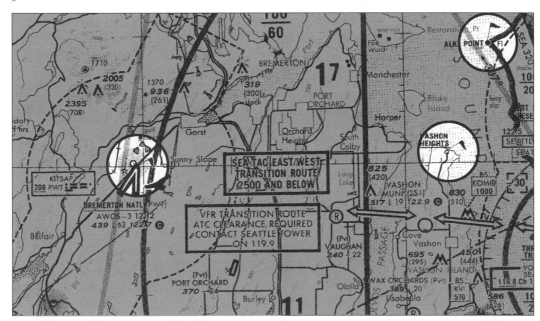

Figure 8-2. Terminal Area Chart, VFR reporting points

While operating in Class B airspace, either landing or passing through, the controller can assign headings and altitudes that will keep you clear of IFR traffic and you must comply; however, if compliance would take you into a cloud you *must* say,

PILOT **"Unable to maintain VFR on that heading [at that altitude], 14W."**

...and the controller will provide alternate instructions. No controller can authorize you to violate the VFR minimums contained in Part 91.

Instrument pilots have to read back to the controller any clearances that include changes in heading or altitude. There is nothing in the regulations that says VFR pilots have to do the same thing, but it makes such good sense that there is no reason not to.

PILOT **"Baron 14W leaving 7,500, descending 4,000"**

PILOT **"Baron 14W, left to 340."**

Once you have been handed off to the control tower operator there is no difference between an airport in Class B airspace and any other controlled airport.

Departing an Airport in the Class B Surface Area

The primary airport in a Class B surface area is a big time operation. There were over 30 such areas in 1994 with more under consideration. These are airports with heavy concentrations of air carrier airplanes and you have to be on your toes. You don't have to be super-pilot, but you do have to stay alert and respond to instructions quickly and accurately without spending too much time talking on the radio.

Everything in the discussion of Class D airspace applies, because this is basically a tower-controlled airport with a few extra requirements. Once again, you should have a Terminal Area Chart on board — if there are any specific requirements they will be on that chart in the form of notes.

If the TAC or the Airport/Facility Directory lists a pre-taxi clearance frequency, keep in mind that this service is intended for IFR flights and it doesn't apply to your VFR flight. Just select the Ground Control frequency and say,

PILOT **"Metro Ground, Cessna 1357X at the south ramp, VFR to Bigburg. Request clearance to operate in Bravo airspace."**

Everyone in the tower knows that you need a clearance to operate in the airspace, but you should not assume that a clearance will come automatically. Don't even accept a "Taxi into position and hold" clearance until you know that operation in Class B airspace has been approved. You will get a discrete transponder code to squawk.

Once again, expect headings and altitudes that will keep you clear of IFR flights until you have crossed the Class B airspace boundary. The tower might say something like,

TOWER "Cessna 1357X, suggest heading 250 [or maintain runway heading], maintain VFR, contact Metro Departure on 123.9."

Don't switch your transponder to the ON position until you are on the runway and in position for takeoff. When the Departure controller can see your transponder return while you are still on the ground, he or she will have accepted responsibility for you before the tower instructs you to change frequencies. If you have to gain a little altitude before Departure can see your return, the "Contact Departure" instruction will be delayed until coordination has been accomplished. Don't change frequencies on your own; if it seems as though you have been forgotten,

PILOT "Do you want 57X to go to Departure?"

…should elicit a frequency change from the tower controller.

When you are departing an airport in Class B airspace most of the work will be done for you. The ground controller will give you a transponder squawk and the tower controller will hand you off to the appropriate terminal controller:

TOWER "Cessna 1357X, contact Bigtown Departure 126.5 now. Have a good day."

PILOT "57X going to departure."

When you are in Class B airspace you must comply with any heading or altitude changes directed by the terminal controller unless you determine that to do so would violate VFR cloud clearance minimums. It is highly unlikely that a controller will assign a specific heading or altitude to a VFR flight, however.

CONTROLLER "Cessna 1357X, turn right heading 340, traffic your ten o'clock a 737 climbing to 12,000 feet."

PILOT "57X has the traffic. Unable 340 due to weather; 270 would keep us clear of clouds."

CONTROLLER "Roger, 57X, turn right heading 270 and advise when you can turn north."

Although you should never turn the safety of your flight over to the controller, what looks like a traffic conflict to you might be part of the controller's master plan.

CONTROLLER "Cessna 1357X, turn left heading 180, descend and maintain 2,500."

PILOT "57X, is the 747 at my two o'clock below 2,500?"

"Roger, 57X, the 747 is for runway 17 left, indicating 2,000 and descending."

PILOT **"57X, left to 180. Leaving 3,000 for 2,500."**

That's a whole lot better than simply following instructions blindly and showing your Christmas tie to the passengers on the 747.

On the reverse side of the terminal area chart you will find VFR flyways that are designed to let you fly through the area with a minimum of radio contact. Look them over, discuss them with your instructor, and use them as much as possible. If you fly the routes shown at the altitudes indicated on the chart you will be safely clear of the big iron. This does not mean that you don't need a clearance to enter the Class B airspace but it does show what you can ask for and almost always get — although it is not a sure thing.

In really congested airspace, such as that around the Los Angeles International Airport, the FAA has designated VFR corridors. Note the difference between a flyway and a corridor: A corridor is not part of the surrounding Class B airspace, and a flyway is. In the case of Los Angeles, the chart shows the altitude, the route of flight, and the frequency to be used to announce the fact that you are in the corridor. No contact with ATC is required or expected. This is not the kind of airspace you want to blunder into unprepared.

Every primary airport with Class B airspace has a control tower, but there is no Class D airspace as such. The terminal controller will hand you off to the tower:

APPROACH **"57X you're following the twin on right base, contact the tower 118.3 now."**

PILOT **"57X going to the tower."**

When departing the primary airport in Class B airspace listen closely to the controller and make sure that you have a clearance to operate in the Class B airspace. If you're not sure, ask. The assignment of a transponder code and a handoff from the tower to the departure controller do not constitute a clearance if you are operating under Visual Flight Rules.

It helps a lot if you say "VFR" as often as possible:

PILOT **"Bigtown Departure, Piper 70497, 1,000 climbing 4,500, VFR to Littleburg."**

DEPART **"497, radar contact, cleared to operate in the Bravo airspace — we had you as an instrument departure."**

Departing From a Satellite Airport Beneath Class B Airspace

Look at almost any Terminal Area Chart and you will see airports that are located outside of the Class B surface area, but beneath a "shelf" in the Bravo airspace. On the sectional chart excerpt, Auburn (Airport J) offers a good example. An airplane departing Auburn heading westbound will run right into Class B airspace and must obtain a clearance into that airspace before takeoff or immediately thereafter:

> PILOT **"Seattle Departure, Piper 70497 off from Auburn VFR to Bremerton, request clearance through your Bravo airspace,"**

…and have that clearance in hand before approaching closer than a mile to the Bravo airspace boundary.

Figure 8-3. Auburn Municipal Airport, Washington

Summary

As airspace goes, Class B is more important to the VFR pilot than any other airspace designation. You absolutely, positively, must hear "Cleared to operate in the Bravo airspace" before entry. If you are not sure, ask. "Radar contact" does not constitute a clearance into Class B airspace. You must maintain VFR and fly any headings and altitudes assigned; if you would lose VFR cloud clearance by doing so, you must inform the controller and ask for an amended clearance.

9 Class A Airspace

It's for the Chosen Few

You won't be operating in Class A airspace unless you have an instrument rating and are operating on an instrument flight plan, so there are no special communication requirements or procedures for VFR flight in Class A airspace.

Occasionally, a VFR pilot who wins the lottery or gets that big promotion buys an airplane that is capable of flying above 18,000 feet and climbs through that altitude in attempt to get above the weather. Almost every Center controller has a story about an exchange with a pilot who has been legally flying in Class A airspace:

> PILOT "Center, are you talking to that Centurion [or Malibu, or 340, or...] at my two o'clock, about my altitude?"

> CENTER "Negative. He's squawking VFR and we're not talking to him. Are you close enough to get his tail number?"

ATC tracks these interlopers to their destinations, of course, and they get a violation.

⑩ Automated Flight Service Stations

Service is Their Middle Name

As a VFR pilot you will be talking to Flight Service Stations frequently, so they deserve coverage in detail.

Automated Flight Service Stations are proliferating like bunny rabbits. At the same time the ability to walk into an FSS to talk to a briefer and look at weather charts is disappearing like an ice cube in the Sahara, although they will welcome you with open arms if you are fortunate enough to find one with easy access from an airport. (Don't bother calling the National Weather Service — they no longer provide pilot briefings.) The AFSS system is set up primarily for pilot access by radio or telephone.

To get the same geographical coverage that they used to get with multiple manned locations, the FAA uses Remote Communication Outlets (RCOS); VORs with voice capability are being phased out.

Air traffic controllers, whether they work in a tower, at a radar facility, or at a Flight Service Station (they all belong to the same union) are at all times alert for incoming calls — that's what they are there for. In most cases the paperwork load at a radar facility is handled by an assistant. Conversely, a Flight Service Station specialist does it all.

Making Contact

All of those RCOs mean that the specialist has a bank of pushbuttons to monitor, and when you call in, one of those buttons flickers faintly. It doesn't flash on and off as your telephone does when you put someone on hold, it just flickers. An initial transmission that includes your position and the facility you are using for communication is essential. If you transmit,

> PILOT "**Riverside Radio, Baron 1014W, over**"

…you present a busy specialist with a puzzle. Which button flickered? If you are at a high enough altitude to reach two remote locations that are assigned the same frequency, both buttons flickered and the specialist needs to know which one to reply on. This is no time for game playing:

> PILOT "**Riverside Radio, Baron 1014W on 122.2 over Dagget**"

— is the way to go.

If you want to communicate through an RCO, you'll find its name in a box, with the name of the controlling FSS beneath it (see the box just west of Paine Field, Airport F on the sectional chart excerpt). In this situation, you transmit on 122.55:

> PILOT "**Seattle Radio, Piper 70497, on 122.55 [give location], extend my flight plan from Sky Harbor to Olympia, new ETA 1830Z.**"

This will work even if the specialist is on the phone or otherwise occupied when your call comes in, because you have eliminated all doubt as to what frequency should be used.

A major drawback of the move to automated Flight Service Stations is that in most cases the specialist can no longer look out of the window and provide a pilot with information about traffic in the pattern. At an AFSS, the specialists sit at banks of computer monitors in darkened rooms without windows, just like air traffic controllers at radar facilities.

Special Use Airspace

The Flight Service Station is your best source of information on the status of Special Use Airspace (SUA) such as Restricted, Warning, and Alert Areas. The FSS specialist also has the latest available information on Military Training Routes (MTRs). I say "latest available" because the military quite frequently changes its plans at the last moment, too late to notify the FSS.

The controlling agency for any given area of SUA is given in the communications panel on sectional charts, and if you want to call the control tower at a military air field to ask if a certain area is "hot" you are free to do so:

> PILOT "**Whidbey Tower, Baron 1014W, what is the status of restricted area R-6701?**"

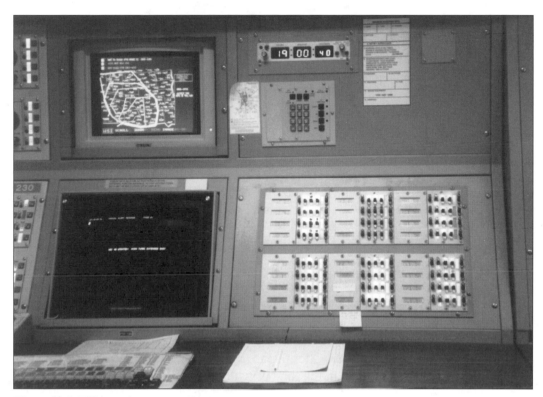

Figure 10-1. FSS console

Calling the FSS will get you exactly the same information:

> PILOT **"Seattle Radio, Baron 1014W over Port Townsend on 122.55, what is the status of R-6701?"**

Military aircraft using MTRs are camouflaged and fast, and are therefore hard to see. Planes flying on routes identified with four-digit numbers (IR 1006, VR 1007) will be flying below 1,500 feet above ground level — in some cases as low as 100 feet above the ground. Routes identified with three-digit numbers (IR 008, VR 009) are flown more than 1,500 feet above ground level, but some segments may be below that altitude.

The military advises the FSS what routes are to be used and the hours during which the route will be hot. Your call to the FSS will be very much like a check on SUA:

> PILOT **"Fort Worth Radio, Baron 1014W, over Childress. What is the status of military route India Romeo 1142?"**

In any event, you should plan to cross military training routes at a 90-degree angle so as to limit your exposure to conflicting military traffic. Military airplanes quite frequently fly in formations that spread out a mile or more from the centerline of the MTR, so paralleling an MTR is a big mistake. Also, if you do catch a glimpse of a military airplane there is probably one or more nearby.

Filing Flight Plans

As soon as you start your student cross-country flights, your instructor begins to drum into your head the need to file VFR flight plans, and to remember to open and close them. The advent of the automated FSS and the proliferation of remote communications sites makes this easy. Dialing 1-800-WX-BRIEF works virtually everywhere.

After you have filed your flight plan (with its proposed departure time) with the FSS specialist, it is held in pending status waiting for you to call and activate it. After making your initial call and establishing communication:

> PILOT "Williamsport Radio, Piper 70497, please open my VFR flight plan from McGinness to Chambersburg at five minutes past the hour."

If you call more than ten minutes after departure, it is important to give the time that you actually took off, rather than the time at which you call the FSS to activate your flight plan, because your filed time en route is calculated from the departure airport to the destination airport.

Air-Filing Flight Plans

Flight Service Stations will accept air-filed flight plans, but they would rather have you do it over the phone to cut down on radio frequency use. You should understand that the specialist has a standard FAA flight plan ready to make the process go as smoothly as possible; it is only necessary for you to transmit the information required to fill in the blocks.

> PILOT "Great Falls Radio, Baron 1014W has a VFR flight plan when you are ready to copy."

> RADIO "This is Great Falls, go ahead."

> PILOT "Great Falls Radio, Baron 1014W: VFR, 1014W, Baron E-55 slant Romeo, 160 knots, Missoula, off at 0800Z, 12,500 feet, V-2,..."

You get the idea — you don't have to read the heading of each block to the specialist, just provide the information that goes in the block on the flight plan form.

Figure 10-2. Flight plan form

Position Reports

The practice of making position reports while on a VFR cross-country has fallen into disuse. If you are receiving radar flight following from an Air Route Traffic Control Center, of course, position reports are unnecessary — the controller knows where you are. If you are not using that service, however, it is in your best interest to make position reports:

> PILOT **"Casper Radio, Cessna 1357X is over Converse County at 15 minutes past the hour, VFR from Casper to Lusk."**

If you fail to arrive at Lusk, the Search-and-Rescue folks can pretty much forget about searching between Casper and Converse County. Search and Rescue is the reason you file flight plans in the first place, so it is in your interest to give potential searchers as much information as possible. Making a pilot report or asking Flight Watch for weather information is a great way to put your position on record.

Many pilots assume that their flight plan is etched in stone and fail to amend it when things don't work out the way they planned. This means that searchers concentrate their efforts along the flight-planned route because they have no way of knowing that the pilot diverted to another route:

PILOT "Seattle Radio, Piper 70497, over Sunnyside at 4,500 feet. I am on a VFR flight plan from Yakima to Olympia via Snoqualmie Pass. Please amend my route to via the Columbia Gorge to the Battle Ground VOR, then direct Olympia and extend my ETA to 1500Z."

Close Your Flight Plan!

Except for Emergency Locator Beacon false alarms, nothing causes more headaches for the Search and Rescue folks than failure to close flight plans upon arrival. If you don't contact the FSS and close out your flight plan, the searchers are going to come looking for you — it's that simple. The S&R business operates on a no-news-is-bad-news basis, and they know that every minute counts to an injured pilot awaiting rescue.

If you have the destination airport in sight and are assured of landing, call the FSS and close your flight plan in the air — but be very sure! Pilots have crashed within a mile or so of the airport after closing their flight plans and no search was begun until relatives began calling for information. If the destination airport has a Remote Communication Outlet, use that or the phone. If you are at a location where 1-800-WX-BRIEF doesn't work, call long distance if you have to, but *close your flight plan!*

Direction Finding Service

Many Flight Service Stations offer direction finding services (check the A/FD — look for VHF-DF). When you call one of these stations and report that you are lost or disoriented, the FSS specialist will ask you to key the push-to-talk switch on your microphone for ten seconds or so — counting from one to ten and back will do the job — and through use of the DF equipment he or she will be able to give you headings to fly toward better weather or an airport. You should use 121.5 MHz (or any FSS or tower frequency) and say MAYDAY in your initial call if you are in a distress situation:

PILOT "Mayday, Mayday, Mayday, any station this is Piper 70497. I'm not sure of my position and I'm running low on fuel."

You will get several answers; respond to the clearest signal.

FSS specialists must be periodically recertified for direction finding duties and that means that they need as much practice as they can get. For that reason, if you are just out tooling around and have 15 minutes or so of free time, call the closest FSS on 122.2 or the RCO frequency listed on your sectional and say:

PILOT "Butte Radio, Cessna 1357X, would you like to give me a practice DF steer?"

They may change you to another frequency so that the DF exercise doesn't conflict with other FSS duties. *Do not* give your location in your initial call; that would take all the challenge out of the problem for the FSS personnel.

Direction finding is not the only trick up the FSS specialist's sleeve — they also practice lost aircraft orientation using VOR and ADF.

Can You Tell Me Where There is a Hole?

In this enlightened age there are still VFR pilots who will fly 100 miles to an area which was reporting overcast skies at the time of departure, hoping against hope that there will be an opening in the clouds through which they can descend. Almost all of them survive, although they create a lot of adrenaline in the pilots and controllers who monitor the situation on the radio. Sometimes they have to turn around and fly back home, sometimes they find a hole through dumb luck, and sometimes they have to call for help.

The Direction Finder service mentioned earlier can help, if there is an airport with VFR weather available, but because radar coverage is so extensive, lost pilots usually end up talking to a radar controller who can vector them to a known VFR area (if one exists) or radar-monitor a descent through the clouds to VFR conditions over water or flat terrain.

The military operates Ground Controlled Approach (GCA) facilities throughout the nation, and they are able to talk pilots right down to the ground. Your best bet, if that hoped-for hole doesn't materialize, is to check with the FSS to learn if there is a GCA available. The military controllers need practice in order to maintain their certification, and solicit the general aviation community for practice approaches. This is something well worth doing with an instructor or safety pilot on board just in case you might need a GCA some day.

Flight Watch

The Enroute Flight Advisory Service, known and addressed as "Flight Watch" has as its sole responsibility the provision of weather information to pilots. A discrete frequency, 122.0 MHz, is assigned to Flight Watch and a specially-trained controller guards that frequency from 0600 until 2200 local time. This frequency is to be used by pilots flying at altitudes up to 17,500 feet MSL; discrete frequencies are available for flights above that altitude (check the A/FD). If you can't make contact, use a regular FSS frequency.

Flight Watch will provide you with weather information pertinent to your flight — that is, weather for your destination and enroute airports. Requests for random or general weather information will be referred to an appropriate FSS frequency. Flight Watch is not to be used for filing flight plans or any other non-weather purpose. It is the means through which pilot reports (PIREPs) are collected and disseminated.

The inside back cover of the Airport/Facility Directory for each geographic region contains a map of Flight Watch stations and their remote outlets.

> PILOT **"Cedar City Flight Watch, Cessna 1357X over Billings, VFR to Bozeman, can I have the latest Bozeman observation and the terminal forecast, please"**

— will work every time. If, after reading this book, you still do not own a copy of the A/FD, simply switching to 122.0 and saying,

> PILOT **"Flight Watch, Cessna 1357X over Billings, over"**

— will get an answer.

Pilot Reports

The *Aeronautical Information Manual* contains explicit instructions on how to provide pilot reports to a Flight Watch specialist (between 2200 and 0600 local) or FSS radio position, and for their benefit you should use the prescribed format. However, they will accept just about anything. If you miss an item they will ask for it. Pilot reports provide critical information to pilots during the flight planning stage, and you should observe the Golden Rule: Do unto others as you would have them do unto you.

If the weather forecast calls for marginal VFR along your route and you are thinking of canceling, wouldn't it be nice to get a PIREP saying that the forecast is wrong and the weather is beautiful? When you are flying in beautiful weather, then, file a pilot report:

> PILOT "**Oakland Flight Watch, Piper 70497 over Fresno at 7,500 feet VFR from Delano to Sacramento. Smooth ride all the way, good VFR at this altitude, lower broken layer between Bakersfield and Visalia.**"

...or, if the tops of the clouds were forecast to be at 12,000 to 15,000 feet, and you are flying behind a 65 horsepower engine, wouldn't it be nice to learn that they are no higher than 7,000 feet?

It's a two-way street — file pilot reports and ask the FSS for pilot reports. Your reports will not only be made available to other pilots, but will also be forwarded to the National Weather Service for use in making and correcting forecasts.

Summary

The network of Flight Service Stations is an asset that is not used often enough by general aviation pilots, for reasons that are not clear to me. Filing and closing flight plans is neither difficult nor onerous; as a search pilot I can tell you that the lack of a destination or route on a missing aircraft makes search planning a matter of playing guessing games.

11   The IFR Communicator

What's the Difference?

In many ways, the procedures and techniques you have learned so far duplicate what you will need to know as you begin training for the instrument rating. The terminology will change a little, but the major difference is that you must be constantly listening for a call from a controller. If you miss a call, the controller must take time away from other pilots to call you again and again. You can't just turn down the volume and enjoy the scenery. Communication is a team effort that involves both the controller and the pilot in achieving the goal of a safe flight. Neither member of the team can afford to sit back and take it easy.

The Hearback Problem

When you receive an instrument clearance on the ground before departure, you are expected to read it back to the controller; when airborne, you are expected to read back those portions of clearances involving altitudes, altitude restrictions, and vectors. We all think of this as a fail-safe method, but it has a fatal flaw — the very human tendency to hear what we expect to hear.

CONTROLLER **"Baron 1014W, turn right heading 330"**

PILOT **"Right to 300, 14W"**

You would expect the controller to pick up that error, wouldn't you? But the controller expected 14W to say 330 and that is what he heard. It works both ways — if a pilot expects a descent to 2,200 feet and is instead cleared to 3,200 feet, it is altogether possible for that pilot to descend through 3,200 feet on the way to 2,200 feet. The hearback problem has been the suspected cause of several accidents and is the proven cause of hundreds of altitude or heading violations.

"I read back the clearance. No adverse word from the controller, so we agreed that we had been cleared..."

"We talked among ourselves that it seemed too early to be given a descent down to 6,000 feet. However, since the controller had not contradicted our readback, we descended..."

"We heard the controller calling ABC 143 four times. We did not answer these calls. Later, we came to believe that she had been trying to reach us (ABC123)."

Silence is Not Agreement

When juggling traffic, controllers must keep a lot of balls in the air at the same time. A controller cannot and does not take the time to monitor the actions of each airplane in the sector. That's why you, as a pilot, have to hold up your end of the implicit controller/pilot partnership for safety. If the controller calls Piper 1357X and you are flying Cessna 1357X (no two airplanes have the same tail number, but controllers can make mistakes as to aircraft models), ask —

PILOT **"Was that for Cessna 1357X?"**

— rather than wait for the controller to finally see the light. Similarly, if you are given a vector in an unexpected direction without explanation ("this is a vector through the localizer for spacing"..."Turn right heading 090 for traffic") don't just sit there waiting for the controller to see and correct the error. Speak up. And help other pilots by exercising the Golden Rule:

PILOT **"Departure, I think the wrong airplane acknowledged your last transmission."**

PILOT **"Center, Baron 1014W read back the wrong altitude."**

I'll Show 'Em!!

There are very, very few shy pilots. Almost all pilots are assertive to some degree and some are downright nasty. If you are heading 270° and the controller says:

CONTROLLER **"Cessna 1357X, turn right heading 240"**

…you could make a 330° right turn (into following traffic?) just to make a point. It's a lot easier to say,

PILOT **"A right turn is the long way around for 57X."**

Occasionally, of course, the controller will want you to turn the long way around — but that will be stated in the directive:

CONTROLLER **"Cessna 1357X, turn right heading 240, the long way around."**

Write It Down

The AIM suggests that pilots keep a written record of all clearances, and forms are available at pilot supply stores for those who don't want to "roll their own." Because route clearances follow a consistent format, let me suggest the old C-R-A-F-T trick. Simply write the letters C, R, A, F, and T vertically along the left-hand edge of a piece of paper; the letters stand for:

Ⓒ learance limit. Usually (but not always) the destination airport.

Ⓡ oute. This might be a series of airways and intersections.

Ⓐ ltitude. This is usually a straight climb but might include restrictions.

Ⓕ requency. This will be Departure Control or Center.

Ⓣ ransponder squawk. Self-explanatory.

If you fly out of one airport regularly, you will be able to fill in most of the blanks even before you start the engine, just based on experience.

Ⓒ *Clearance Limit*

If you have filed an IFR flight plan from Dallas to Houston, you have a 90 percent chance of being right if you write HOUSTON, because your clearance will probably begin "ATC clears Baron 1014W to the Houston airport via…" ATC used to clear flights to enroute intersections and have them enter holding patterns at those intersections until traffic permitted them to proceed to their destinations. Now, ATC holds flights on the ground rather than in the air. That's why there is such a small chance of being cleared to an enroute fix.

Ⓡ *Route*

If you have filed a preferred route to your destination (see the Airport/Facility Directory), you may hear "cleared as filed." If your departure airport has a published Standard Instrument Departure (SID), you will hear "…via the Lakes One Departure, GONZO, V-15…".

A busy airport may have several instrument departures, with the SID assigned being a function of which way you are going. You could monitor ground or clearance delivery to see what type of departure is being assigned to other flights going your way, or you could simply call the tower on the phone and ask. In any case, you should be able write a route after the R that would require only a little bit of editing as your clearance is transmitted to you.

Ⓐ *Altitude*

If there is an altitude restriction in the published SID, the controller need not repeat it in the clearance. For example, at Boeing Field the NEEDLE FIVE departure tells the pilot to maintain 2,000 feet and expect higher within 6 miles. In this case I would write 2,000 after the A, followed by an upward slanting arrow with "6mi" written under it, followed by the filed altitude. If, upon receipt, the clearance to a higher altitude is something other than the filed altitude, all I have to do is draw a line through it and write in the new assignment.

Ⓕ *Frequency*

You should be able to determine the Departure Control frequency in use by monitoring the tower for a few minutes. Or look at the A/FD — there probably aren't more than two frequencies; write them both down and draw a line through the one that you are not assigned.

(T) *Transponder*

If you can predetermine your transponder code you should buy a bunch of lottery tickets. When the Center computer coughs up your clearance it assigns a code. There is no way in the world to anticipate it, but hey! It's only four digits!

Another Handy Trick

For use while en route, make four columns on a 3x5 card headed FREQ, ALT, HDG, and SQUAWK. Every time you are assigned a new frequency, altitude, heading, or squawk, write it in the appropriate column and draw a line through the previous one. That way you can always read the last assignment if you need it and you have the current assignment handy.

Some pilots use the rotatable azimuth on the ADF to remember altitudes — set 40 at the top if your assigned altitude is 4,000 feet, etc.

Ready to Copy

So there you are, with most of your clearance already written down and a pencil ready to correct only those items that differ from your best guess — that's a whole lot better than trying to copy a clearance from scratch on a clean piece of paper:

> PILOT **"Oakland Clearance Delivery, Cessna 1357X is ready to copy"**

> CLEARANCE DELIVERY **"57X, your clearance is on request."**

What does that mean? Do you have to request it again or something? No, it means that when you taxied out, one of the controllers in the tower picked up the phone and told the Center controller that you would be calling for your clearance soon (requested your clearance). Just as soon as it comes out of the computer, it will be ready for you.

By the way, never fail to mention the fact that you are going IFR to everyone who might be interested:

> PILOT **"Oakland Ground, Cessna 1357X at the general aviation ramp, IFR to Seattle."**

> PILOT **"Oakland Tower, Cessna 1357X ready for takeoff on 27R at Alfa One, IFR to Seattle."**

Excerpt from Callback Newsletter

"Heading 330 was interpreted as a clearance to climb to FL330…"

It doesn't happen often, but if a pilot doesn't emphasize the fact that the flight is IFR and the weather is good, the tower can issue a takeoff clearance and not realize that it is an IFR flight until the pilot says,

PILOT "Tower, do you want me to change over to Departure Control now?"

That's because at busy towers, the local controller doesn't get involved in the issuing of clearances or taxi instructions.

Away From the Big City

What if you are departing from a smaller airport, one that doesn't have such niceties as Standard Instrument Departures and terminal radar? The word from here is: *carry sectional charts!* You'll probably be getting your clearance from a Remote Communication Outlet or over the phone from the Flight Service Station, and it is going to be something like this:

CONTROLLER "ATC clears Piper 70497 to the Missoula Airport as filed, maintain runway heading, when able proceed direct Mullan Pass VOR, maintain 9,000 feet, reaching 6,000 feet contact Salt Lake Center 128.35, squawk 6723. Clearance void if not off by 20 minutes past the hour."

What does "when able" mean? The Pilot/Controller Glossary definition is not very helpful. As a practical matter, it means "when you can proceed without hitting anything…" It doesn't mean "when able to receive Mullan Pass," because it might be possible to get a signal and still be below the tops of the mountains, and it certainly doesn't mean "as soon as you are off the ground." Now you can see why I emphasized the need for a sectional chart; you have to provide your own terrain clearance until you reach 6,000 feet (in this case), and you need to know where the mountains are.

What if you hear Salt Lake City on 128.35 as you are climbing through 5,000 feet and decide to give them an early call? The controller says "radar contact." Now who is in charge of terrain clearance? You are! Until you have reached the controller's minimum instrument altitude (something that the controller knows but you don't), and the controller gives you a vector, the controller has no responsibility to keep you away from the rocks. It's pretty easy to figure that 6,000 feet is the MIA in that controller's sector. The job of an air traffic controller is to keep IFR airplanes separated from one another, period. ATC will not give you a vector until you are so high that there is nothing available for you to hit except other airplanes, and they won't allow that.

On the Way

Once you are airborne, instrument flight is just a matter of flying headings and altitudes assigned. Except for handoffs from one sector to another or from a terminal facility (Approach/Departure) to an enroute facility (Center), you won't have much communicating to do. Be sure to include your altitude in any contact with a new controller:

> DEPART "Baron 1014W, Orlando Departure, contact Jacksonville Center 127.55. Good day."

> PILOT "Going to 127.55, 14W"

…keep the Departure frequency written down, or on the #2 radio, just in case.

> PILOT "Jacksonville Center, Baron 1014W, level 6,000."

> CENTER "14W, Jacksonville, radar contact, altimeter 30.11."

Sectorization

Both terminal and en route airspace is divided into horizontal and vertical sectors (*see* Figure 11-1 on the next page). A controller cannot let you leave his or her airspace and enter an adjoining sector without coordinating the handoff with the new sector's controller. During the quiet hours, staffing levels may call for one controller to take over more than one contiguous sector, while during the morning and evening rush each sector will have a controller assigned. I only mention this to explain why you talk to only one controller at one time of day and to several at another time of day.

Changing Altitude

The English language has two troublesome prepositions: to and for. They are troublesome because they sound like two and four. You can eliminate any confusion by simply omitting the prepositions:

> PILOT "Cessna 1357X, leaving 4,000, climbing 6,000."

> PILOT "Cessna 1357X, leaving 8,000 descending 4,000."

Figure 11-1. This chart is no longer up-to-date, but it illustrates how sectorization works.

Approach Clearances

As you near your destination, the words you are waiting to hear are "cleared for the approach." Until you hear those words you must maintain the last assigned altitude. Once you have your clearance and you are on a segment of a published approach procedure (approach plate), you can begin your descent. On the plate itself, each segment has a course and a minimum altitude assigned, so when you hear the approach clearance you can leave the last assigned altitude and descend to the altitude for the published segment you are on. I don't want to steal your instrument instructor's thunder, but if you fly exactly on the black lines and at the published minimum altitude you are not going to hit anything.

Unlike the brief clearances you have received en route, requiring only that you acknowledge a change in altitude or heading, an approach clearance is a paragraph. This is the clearance for the ILS approach to runway 13R at Boeing Field:

> [APPROACH] **"Baron 1014W turn left heading 100, intercept the localizer and proceed inbound, cleared for the ILS approach to 13 Right, maintain 2,200 until established on the glide slope, contact the tower 120.6 at NOLLA."**

Now don't let me talk you out of writing the whole clearance down and reading it back word for word (although by the time you wrote half of it down the controller would be saying "14W, did you receive your approach clearance?...Baron 1014W, Boeing Tower..." and generally wondering if you had fallen asleep).

I told you earlier that when airborne, only changes in heading and altitude need be read back. That's still good advice, but in this case it should be expanded upon a little.

> [PILOT] **"1014W, left to 100, cleared for the approach, tower at NOLLA."**

What's wrong with that? You were already at 2,200 (I've done this a few hundred times), so there was no change in altitude. You read back the heading change and acknowledged the approach clearance, and the tower frequency is printed on the approach plate.

It is not unusual for a student to ignore the approach plate and copy the tower frequency wrong:

> [PILOT] **"...and contact tower 123.6 at NOLLA, 497"**

> [APPROACH] **"Negative, 497, the tower frequency is 120.6 — 120.6"**

> [PILOT] **"Roger, approach, contact tower on 120.6, 497."**

Just how well do you think 497 was doing at steering 100, maintaining 2,200 feet, and waiting for the ILS needle to center while getting that straightened out? Probably flew right through the localizer (the beam that aligns airplanes with the runway). Why not read the frequency directly from the approach plate and be done with it?

My point is that you need not read back every word that is transmitted by the controller. I hate to tell you this, but you will hear professional pilots flying for air carriers and corporations respond to a lengthy clearance with "We'll do all that." That is going too far, in my opinion.

Lost Communications

When you prepare for the instrument pilot written exam, and possibly during the oral portion of your practical test, you will have to know what FAR 91.185 requires of a pilot on an IFR flight plan who has suffered a loss of two-way radio communications: set your transponder to 7600, fly at the highest of (1) the altitude assigned in the last ATC clearance received, (2) the Minimum Enroute Altitude for the route segment you are on, or (3) the altitude you have been told to expect in a further clearance. You are also expected to follow the route assigned in your last clearance; the direct route from the point of failure to the fix, route, or airway specified in a vector clearance; or your flight planned route. FAR 91.185 also establishes a means of determining when to begin the approach at your destination relative to your estimated time of arrival.

The unofficial word from Center and Terminal controllers across the country is this: When you arrive at your destination, perform the instrument approach procedure of your choice without delay. Don't get involved in holding at a fix until a predetermined time has elapsed, just get the airplane on the ground. The ATC folks know that you have no communication capability and have sterilized the airspace around the destination airport so that it is all yours. Any delay you insert into the situation will simply further delay those flights holding in the air or on the ground, waiting for you to land.

12 Now That You Know the System...

Teamwork

I hope that this book has encouraged you to pay more attention to the way you communicate as a pilot. The most important message I want you to take away from this text is this: Aviation communications is a team effort. The folks at the Flight Service Stations, the terminal radar facilities, and the enroute traffic control centers want you to complete your flight safely every bit as much as you do.

When All Else Fails

Remember that the microphone is not a flight control, and that for a VFR pilot there is no such thing as loss of communication. Many pilots fly happily without any radios at all. If your radio/mike/speaker/headset fizzles out in a cloud of acrid smoke you have a lot of options. Setting your transponder to 7600 will alert the world at large to the fact that you cannot communicate normally; this will give controllers a "heads up" if your destination is in Class D airspace.

Section 4-42 of the *Aeronautical Information Manual* covers the procedures a VFR pilot should use to join the traffic pattern at an airport in Class D airspace. Basically, you are to remain outside of or above the Class D surface area until you have determined the direction of traffic flow, and then join the pattern while watching for light signals. You can see how squawking 7600 ahead of time would help the controllers in this situation.

My preference would be to land at an uncontrolled airport and contact the destination control tower by phone, giving your airplane type and color, your estimated time of arrival, and the direction from which you will be approaching. That lets the controller advise other pilots in the pattern of your position and intentions when you come into view.

4-42. Communications With Tower When Aircraft Transmitter or Receiver or Both are Inoperative

a. Arriving Aircraft—

1. Receiver inoperative—If you have reason to believe your receiver is inoperative, remain outside or above the Class D surface area until the direction and flow of traffic has been determined; then, advise the tower of your type aircraft, position, altitude, intention to land, and request that you be controlled with light signals. (Reference—Traffic Control Light Signals, paragraph 4-62). When you are approximately 3 to 5 miles from the airport, advise the tower of your position and join the airport traffic pattern. From this point on, watch the tower for light signals. Thereafter, if a complete pattern is made, transmit your position downwind and/or turning base leg.

2. Transmitter inoperative—Remain outside or above the Class D surface area until the direction and flow of traffic has been determined; then, join the airport traffic pattern. Monitorthe primary local control frequency as depicted on Sectional Charts for landing or traffic information, and look for a light signal which may be addressed to your aircraft. During hours of daylight, acknowledge tower transmissions or light signals by rocking your wings. At night, acknowledge by blinking the landing or navigation lights. To acknowledge tower transmissions during daylight hours, hovering helicopters will turn in the direction of the controlling facility and flash the landing light. While in flight, helicopters should show their acknowledgement of receiving a transmission by making shallow banks in opposite directions.

At night, helicopters will acknowledge receipt of transmissions by flashing either the landing or the search light.

3. Transmitter and receiver inoperative—Remain outside or above the Class D surface area until the direction and flow of traffic has been determined; then, join the airport traffic pattern and maintain visual contact with the tower to receive light signals. Acknowledge light signals as noted above.

b. Departing Aircraft—If you experience radio failure prior to leaving the parking area, make every effort to have the equipment repaired. If you are unable to have the malfunction repaired, call the tower by telephone and request authorization to depart without two-way radio communications. If tower authorization is granted, you will be given departure information and requested to monitor the tower frequency or watch for light signals as appropriate. During daylight hours, acknowledge tower transmissions or light signals by moving the ailerons or rudder. At night, acknowledge by blinking the landing or navigation lights. If radio malfunction occurs after departing the parking area, watch the tower for light signals or monitor tower frequency.

4-42b NOTE—Refer to FAR Part 91.129 and Part 91.125.

Figure 12-1. AIM paragraph 4-42

You could try this if your destination airport was in Class C airspace, although communication is the heart and soul of that class of airspace, and you are not supposed to enter it without talking to ATC. The worst thing that could happen is refusal to let you enter the airspace. Don't even think about it if Class B airspace is involved.

In Conclusion…

Controllers don't play "gotcha!" and they don't expect perfection. If you are confused or puzzled by a clearance or instruction, don't do anything until you have asked for clarification (however, instructions like "Turn right *immediately!*" should be obeyed without hesitation). "What do you want me to do? — I don't understand," is a phrase that you won't find in many texts, but it will sure work when you need it. And don't forget that old standby, "Unable."

You now have the information you need to communicate competently and confidently in the National Airspace System. I wish you blue skies, tailwinds, and a clear frequency when you need it.

Appendix A
Communications Facilities

Airport Advisory Area ⬚FSS

At airports that have a Flight Service Station on the field, FSS personnel will provide traffic advisories to pilots operating within ten miles of the airport; this is the Airport Advisory Area. The Sectional Chart Legend indicates that 123.6 MHz should be used for this purpose. Note that the number of Flight Service Stations where personnel have the time or capability to look out of the window is rapidly dwindling as the move to automation continues.

Aeronautical Advisory Service ⬚UNICOM

This is the official name for what all pilots know as UNICOM. The frequency for UNICOM is in the Airport/Facility Directory (A/FD) under the city listing, as well as on sectional charts in the airport data block. UNICOM stations are operated by airport businesses as a service to pilots and have no official status — do not expect official weather reports or takeoff/landing clearances from UNICOM. In fact, don't be surprised if no one answers your call. The UNICOM frequency is, of course, the Common Traffic Advisory Frequency at an airport with a UNICOM, whether anyone is monitoring the frequency or not.

Air Route Traffic Control Center (CENTER) ⬚CENTER

These enroute radar facilities exist to maintain separation between IFR flights and between IFR flights and known VFR flights. Centers will provide VFR traffic advisories on a workload-permitting basis. Center frequencies are found in the A/FD and on instrument enroute charts; in a pinch, you could call the nearest Flight Service Station and ask for the Center frequency in your area.

Approach/Departure Control [APPROACH] / [DEPART]

These are positions at a terminal radar facility (also called a TRACON), responsible for the handling of IFR flights to and from the primary airport. Where Class B airspace exists, these are the controllers that you call for clearance to operate in that airspace. Frequencies are found in the Airport/Facilities Directory (A/FD) under the city name, on sectional charts in the communications panel, and on terminal area charts.

Note: There are some combined tower/approach control facilities that do not have radar. You find the appropriate frequency in the same way, and the only difference you will notice is that the approach controller will ask for frequent position reports over known landmarks so that you can be separated from other known traffic.

Automatic Terminal Information Service (ATIS) [ATIS]

This is a continuous broadcast of an audio tape prepared by an ATC controller that contains wind direction and velocity, temperature, altimeter setting, runway and approach in use, and other information of interest to pilots such as runway or taxiway restriction, obstructions in the area, etc. The ATIS frequency is found in the A/FD under the city name, on sectional charts in the airport data block and in the communications panel, and on terminal area charts.

Clearance Delivery [CLEARANCE DELIVERY]

This is a position in the control tower responsible for transmitting instrument clearances to IFR flights. The clearance delivery frequency is found on instrument approach procedure charts. At those airports where a pilot must copy the instrument clearance before taxiing, the notation Cpt, meaning "pre-taxi clearance," is included on the instrument approach procedure charts. At airports in Class B and C airspace where a transponder code must be assigned to each flight, the ATIS will direct pilots to contact Clearance Delivery (or Ground Control, if there is no Clearance Delivery position at that airport) for a clearance which will include the transponder code and departure instructions. The ATIS broadcast will include the frequency to use.

Common Traffic Advisory Frequency (CTAF) [FSS] / [TOWER] / [UNICOM]

Every civil airport has a Common Traffic Advisory Frequency, found in the A/FD and on sectional charts in the airport data block. The purpose of the CTAF is to provide a single frequency that pilots in the area can use to either contact the controlling facility or broadcast their position and intention to other pilots. The CTAF is found in the A/FD and on sectional charts in the airport data block followed by a white C on a blue or magenta background. At airports without a tower, a Flight Service Station, or UNICOM, the CTAF is 122.9, the MULTICOM frequency.

Enroute Flight Advisory Service (Flight Watch) [FLIGHT WATCH]

The Enroute Flight Advisory Service (EFAS) is a position at a Flight Service Station with responsibility for handling weather inquiries from pilots in flight. It operates from 0600-2200 local time and uses 122.00 MHz for flights operating up to 17,500 feet MSL. Discrete frequencies are assigned for flights operating between 18,000 feet and 45,000 feet MSL; these frequencies (and a map of EFAS outlets) can be found on the inside back cover of the A/FD.

(Automated) Flight Service Station [FSS]

Flight Service Stations exist to provide information and services to pilots. The FAA is consolidating the FSS system into a relatively small number of Automated Flight Service Stations (see Chapter 10). FSS frequencies are found on sectional charts and in the A/FD both under the city name and in a separate listing of AFSS frequencies. On sectionals, frequencies will be found listed above VOR frequency boxes and, when remoted, in separate blue boxes. Read the Sectional Chart Legend carefully — some frequencies are not listed, but their existence is indicated by the thickness of the lines forming the box.

Ground Control [GROUND]

At tower-controlled airports, Ground Control is a position in the tower responsible for controlling aircraft taxiing to and from the runways. Where parallel runways exist, the Ground Controller has no responsibility for the area between the runways — that belongs to the tower, or local, controller. Ground Control frequencies are found in the A/FD under the city name.

Hazardous In-flight Weather Advisory Service (HIWAS) HIWAS

HIWAS is a continuous broadcast of forecast hazardous weather conditions on selected navigational aids. HIWAS has no communication capability; that is, a Flight Service Station cannot break into the HIWAS broadcast to transmit to pilots. VORs that broadcast HIWAS information can be identified on sectional charts by a blue square in the lower right-hand corner of the VOR frequency box. In the A/FD, the notation HIWAS will appear in the airport listing under "Radio Aids to Navigation."

MULTICOM MULTICOM

The MULTICOM frequency is 122.9 MHz and is intended for use by pilots operating at airports with no radio facilities. The self-announce procedures in the *Aeronautical Information Manual* are especially valuable at these airports. In the A/FD, airports where MULTICOM should be used show 122.9 as the CTAF. On sectional charts, the frequency 122.9 is followed by a white C on a dark background, indicating that it is the CTAF.

Tower TOWER

The controller responsible for operations on the runways and in the Class B, C, or D airspace surrounding the airport is officially the "local" controller, although "tower" is the commonly used designation. The tower frequency is found on sectional and terminal control area charts in the airport data block and the communications panel, and also in the Airport/Facility Directory under the city listing. When the tower is not in operation, the CTAF is still the tower frequency. The tower controller "owns" the surface of the active runway or runways and any taxiways between active runways, as well as the airspace up to (typically) 2,500 feet AGL and out to the boundaries shown on the chart.

B Appendix B
Airspace Definitions

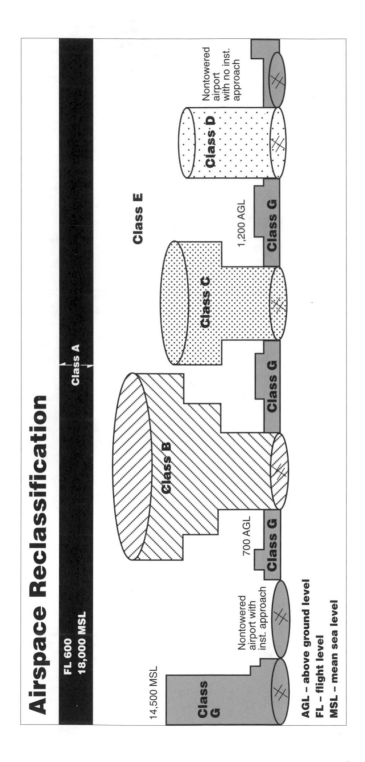

Airspace Reclassification

Airspace	Class A	Class B	Class C	Class D	Class E	Class G
Entry Requirements	ATC clearance	ATC clearance	Prior two-way communications	Prior two-way communications	Prior two-way communications* or nothing	Prior two-way communications* or nothing
Minimum Pilot Qualifications	Instrument Rating	Private or Student certification. Location dependent.	Student certificate	Student certificate	Student certificate	Student certificate
Two-way Radio Communications	Yes	Yes	Yes	Yes	Yes*	Yes*
Special VFR allowed	No	Yes	Yes	Yes	Yes	N/A
VFR Visibility Minimum	N/A	3 statute miles	3 statute miles	3 statute miles	3 statute miles	1 statute mile
VFR Minimum Distance from Clouds	N/A	Clear of clouds	500' below, 1,000' above, 2,000' horizontal	500' below, 1,000' above, 2,000' horizontal	500' below, 1,000' above, 2,000' horizontal	Clear of clouds
VFR Aircraft Separation	N/A	All	IFR	Runway Operations	None	None
Traffic Advisories	Yes	Yes	Yes	Workload permitting	Workload permitting	Workload permitting
Airport Application	N/A	• Radar • Instrument Approaches • Weather • Control Tower • High Density	• Radar • Instrument Approaches • Weather • Control Tower	• Instrument Approaches • Weather • Control Tower	• Instrument Approaches • Weather	• Control Tower or nothing

*Only if a temporary tower, or control tower is present, which is the exception.

I Index

Say Again, Please
A Focus Series Book

Technical Editor	Jackie Spanitz
Editor	Jennie Trerise
Art Director	Dora McClurkin Muir
Design/Production	Jennifer Shontz

Produced at ASA's Graphic Design & Publications Department
in Times, Helvetica, Helvetica Light, and Helvetica Black
using Microsoft Word, Aldus FreeHand, Adobe Photoshop and Aldus PageMaker.

Product names are trademarks or registered trademarks of their respective holders.